Southern Grandmother Stories

Vicki H. Moss

Cover photo by Vicki H. Moss

Cover Fonts are Chopin Script and Constantina
Interior Title Font is Constantina
Body Text Font is Times New Roman

Scripture references are taken from the *King James Version* of the Bible.

Southern Grandmother Stories
ISBN: 978-1-60495-107-9

Copyright © 2025 by Vicki H. Moss. Published in the U.S.A. by Grace Publishing, Broken Arrow, Oklahoma. All rights reserved. No part of this book may be reproduced in any form or by any electronic or mechanical means, including information storage and retrieval systems, without permission in writing from the author, except as provided by U.S.A. Copyright law.

Dedication

I DEDICATE THIS BOOK to all of the intriguing people the Lord has introduced me to. If it weren't for His placing me in their paths, or them in mine, I wouldn't have the interesting and sometimes absorbing stories that might possibly encourage others; some stories that are happy and uplifting, some sad yet reflective, and some with—hopefully—insightful takeaways.

Acknowledgments

MANY OF THESE STORIES were first published in the *Moments* series published by Grace Publishing, and I'd like to posthumously acknowledge my dear friend, Yvonne Lehman, for sparking this series to life. Though Yvonne is no longer with us, the idea for compiling God moments into a book came from a gathering of writers catching up on one another's lives since the previous Blue Ridge Mountains Christian Writers Conference near Asheville, North Carolina.

While together in a sitting area of one of the campus hotels, these writers regaled one another with their God stories—how God had helped or intervened in their lives. Yvonne agreed that a compilation of their stories would make for an interesting and uplifting book—the first one titled *Divine Moments*.

With the help of Terri Kalfas of Grace Publishing, the *Moments* series blossomed into being with many more compilations published over the years, with proceeds going to Franklin Graham's organization, Samaritan's Purse. Since Yvonne's passing, Terri has taken up the mantle and carried forth with the compiling of Christian writers' God stories, continuing to publish these delightful books that have inspired so many. So thank you, Terri, for your efforts in helping to get the word out—that God is still working in our lives today. He has never left us, nor will He ever.

In this book, I've gathered many of my Moments stories in one place with a few additional stories so my descendants will know what their Southern grandmother experienced in her walk with the Lord.

For those kind readers interested in a few God stories, I hope you enjoy!

~Vicki

Stories first published in the Divine Moments series* compiled and edited by Yvonne Lehman and Terri Kalfas—published by Grace Publishing.

Divine Moments
 "Roach Coach Angel"
 "Two Old Women"

Spoken Moments
 "The Humbling Words"
 "Words of Validation"

Precious, Precocious Moments
 "A Battle with the Mouse King"
 "Cat Funerals"
 "The Potholder"

Stupid Moments
 "From Fourteen-Karat Mind to the Mind of Christ"
 "I Could Have Been a Contender If I Hadn't Had a Jesus Crush"

* *Why? Titanic Moments*
 "Together in the Daybreak"

Loving Moments
 "If Only by Toe-Touch"

Cool-inary Moments
 "Delight Comes in Layers"
 "Keep It Moist"

Moments with Billy Graham
  "Turning the Knob for Billy"

Personal Titanic Moments
  "Laying My Watery Ghosts to Rest"

Romantic Moments
  "Give Me the Exclusive"
  "I Am My Beloved's and My Beloved Is Mine"
  "Romance on the River"

Can, Sir!
  "When Joy Finally Comes"

Lost…and Found
  "Something Happened on the Backside of the Boondocks"
  "Searching for the Lost"

Treasured Moments
  "Never So Thrilled to See a Toilet"
  "Come What May"

Table of Contents

Introduction 9
1. Peony Tea Parties 13
2. Roach Coach Angel 20
3. Two Old Women 24
4. Delight Comes in Layers 30
5. Keep It Moist 34
6. Turning the Knob for Billy 39
7. Give Me the Exclusive 46
8. I Am My Beloved's and My Beloved Is Mine 49
9. Romance on the River 54
10. A Strange Thing Happened on the Backside
    of a Boondock 58
11. Questionable Vacations 68
12. Laying My Watery Ghosts to Rest 77
13. Together in the Daybreak 83
14. When Joy Finally Comes 90
15. The Humbling Words 96
16. Words of Validation 102
17. A Battle with the Mouse King 110
18. Cat Funerals 116
19. The Potholder 118

20. From 14-Karat Mind to the Mind of Christ 121
21. I Could Have Been a Contender if I Hadn't Had
    a Jesus Crush 129
22. If Only by Toe-Touch 136
23. A Day for Me 142
24. Searching for the Lost 146
25. Broken with Character 150
26. A Pinch of Clay 155
27. Breaking Points 160
28. Swimming to Cuba 169
29. Never So Thrilled to See a Toilet 175
30. The Rack of Ribs That Got Away 178
31. From One Who Loves Her Country 183
32. Spelunking My Way to Jesus 191
33. Come What May 197
34. Little Joker 203
35. Never Judge an Orange by the Fuzz 217
36. Paying Peonies Forward 226
About the Author 234

Introduction

When my daughter began teaching my eldest grandchild, Hayden, rules and boundaries, she would say, "That's not available to you right now." So, at an early age, Hayden learned the meaning of *available*. Definition of available: Able to be used or obtained; at someone's disposal; present and ready for use; at hand; accessible.

To simplify the definition, for Hayden "not available" meant *you can't have it.*

Therefore, by the time she was two years old, Hayden knew what it meant when she wasn't allowed to play with markers for drawing, or use her iPad for games and shows. To limit her time on a sometimes mind-numbing device like an iPad, the machine simply was *not available.*

It wasn't long until Hayden discovered another meaning of available. When I would first walk through Hayden's front door for a visit, which usually meant I would also be spending a night or two, after jumping into my arms with little girl squeals and hugs and kisses, Hayden would tentatively ask, "Lovie, are you available tonight?" That meant she wanted to sleep with me in my bed. Along with at least forty-eleven dolls and stuffed animals—the worst of which was a cat that meowed and purred if it was bumped by a knee in the middle of the night. Then there was the nightlight that she insisted had to be on because it projected stars on the ceiling for about 10 minutes. And of course there had to be soothing music. With barely enough room left in the queen-sized bed, being kicked in the middle of the night was a given, along with having my hair yanked when little hands got caught in my tresses. Sleeping with this Grandee was an adventure.

Of course, I could never turn Hayden's request down because she was afraid of the dark. If my bunking with her gave her and her parents a good night's sleep, if I answered her requests after a couple of books had been read and after a few "Lovie stories" had been told, I was more than willing to help everyone out. I could always catch up on my sleep when I returned home. But sleeping with Hayden also meant I had to go to bed at a quarter of eight to try to get her relaxed and sleepy by eight o'clock. In the winter, this early bedtime wasn't so bad. In summer, when the sun doesn't set until 9 P.M. and there's still daylight outside and I could still be writing or reading, the early bedtime was more of a sacrifice. As a grandmother who loves her grandchildren, this was a sacrifice I was always more than willing to make, but not only that, it gave me time to comfort and counsel and help reassure Hayden that Jesus was always with her and there was no need to feel afraid. All she had to do was call on Him when she became frightened.

After a short season of Hayden asking me if I was available to sleep with her (in the beginning of her asking, she was afraid I would say no) we soon made a game of this request. Shortly after I'd arrived at her house, sometimes I would be the first to have a stern and serious look on my face and ask, "Hayden, I need to know something." Then with a mischievous look I added, "Are you available tonight?" I could see a smile spread from ear to ear as she giggled and replied, "Yes, Lovie. I *am* available!" From then on, it became our special game after an initial greeting.

A couple of years later, when Hayden was four years old, I planned another visit to her home. Thinking about seeing Hayden (and later her sisters, Harper and Hope), I immediately thought about our "are you available" greeting. I had to smile when I visualized her face lighting up from happiness knowing she would have someone sleeping next to her in the dark after her nightlight of stars on the ceiling automatically cut off.

Later, with all three grandchildren in my bed, the Lovie stories continued.

During my musings about these grandmother storytelling times, the ultimate Available One, popped into my mind. Jesus. And I thanked the good Lord that I don't have to wait for a physical visit from Him to talk with Him and be comforted. He is available at all times, and unlike trying to make an appointment with a king or head of state, I can waltz right into the throne room where He sits at the right hand of God at any time with my praise and prayers of petition. Though I don't visually see Him, I know He's there. No matter what is on my mind I can bend the knee before my almighty God and be with Jesus no matter the time of day. I can rest assured knowing this because He has already told those who believe in Him, *"Lo, I am with you always, even unto the end of the world. Amen."* Matthew 28:20

Even when it's difficult to believe this with terrorist attacks all around us and wars and rumors of war, Isaiah 54:10 tells us *the mountains shall depart, and the hills be removed; but my kindness shall not depart from thee, neither shall the covenant of my peace be removed, saith the Lord that hath mercy on thee.*

And since God is the Almighty who cannot lie, I can believe that He is at hand and at my disposal; present and ready for use. God is accessible. With blessed assurance, my Lord is not only available, Jesus is mine!

With that said, I hope you enjoy reading about some of my Southern Grandmother stories, times when God was "available" in my life and made His presence known. I've shared many of these stories with all three grandchildren throughout the years when they've said, "Tell us a story, Lovie!"

Along with the storytelling, one of the things I hope I've instilled in my grandchildren is that God is a God who does not lie. His promises were not only for those who lived in ancient times, they also hold true for those of us who live in the modern world. And because of that if they are attentive to the Holy Spirit's guidance they, too, can also walk with Him to have their own Godcident stories.

God is not a man that he should lie, neither the son of man, that he should repent: hath he said, and shall he not do it? or hath he spoken, and shall he not make it good? Numbers 23:19

...in hope of eternal life, which God, that cannot lie, promised before the world began. Titus 1:2

...by two immutable things, in which it was impossible for God to lie.... Hebrews 6:18

~ 1 ~
Peony Tea Parties

Coming from a line of women who loved peonies, pansies, and petunias, it was a given I would love these flowers as well. Pansies are a perky, short-lived perennial. Planted in the fall, they weather winter well and look beautiful throughout spring until southern summer heat turns them leggy and scraggly. That's when petunias make a garden pop because they love to hang out in the sunshine.

However, peonies—they are a flower of a different sort. With outrageous, fat blossoms, they have been the May divas of my gardens for decades. They come in lots of colors including yellows, corals, reds, medium pinks, pale pinks, white with a drizzle of red in the centers, and more—and sometimes they are the bane of my existence since I never know which week they might think about blooming. Usually it's late spring to early summer. Where I live, most times they bloom the second or third week in May. They fooled me one year and bloomed the first week in May.

Then if they do decide to bloom in a timely manner and a thunderstorm strikes—so much for an outdoor peony tea party because the peony blooms are blasted about hither, thither, and yon and tend to look bedraggled and worn out from raindrop thrashings.

Most herbaceous peonies need support because their blooms are heavy and bow down as though they are worshipping their Creator. Sounds like a fussy plant; however, I've found them extremely easy to grow. Pop them in the ground, usually in the fall. And water when needed—especially during hot weather until they get established. Then wait a couple to three years and you can count on humongous pom-pom blooms. The plant's life span can be up to 100 years.

Peony plants begin to stir about ground level in late winter, or sometimes March. After the lush green leaves bush out, the ants must talk about the peony bud debuts beginning in mid to late April. I'm sure there are ant conversations that go something like this: "We must protect the peony buds in a few weeks!" and "Yes! I can't wait to eat the peony's nectar!" and "Just remember when you're gorging on the sugary nectar, don't forget to attack the bud-eating pests," and "Protect the peony buds at all cost—more sugar for thee and me!"

Then come May in Tennessee's Zone 7, a bud watch is on for the peony gardeners as the buds grow larger and larger and finally begin to slowly open up to reveal their petals. If the neighbors aren't out I sometimes squeal a tad to see these beauties unfurl their layers and layers of petal softness.

When the grandchildren were younger and not as involved in sports and other activities, I would tell my daughter, "Do not plan one thing for the second or third week in May. The peonies might bloom and that's when we must be prepared for the Peony Tea Party. I have darling long garden party dresses ready and they can wear some of my hats."

What parties we have had and will have again out in the

Enchanted Garden surrounded by Siberian iris, cat mint and rose blooms waiting to burst forth while a lovely peony arrangement graces the center of the table surrounded by small finger sandwiches, cookies, strawberries dipped in chocolate, and decorated cupcakes in small clay pots with frogs and handmade marzipan mushrooms painted with food coloring! On one side of the table, sits a cut-glass pitcher of cold iced watermelon tea to be poured into small pink goblets that sit next to folded cloth napkins adorned by tiny watering can napkin rings. Of course, a baby doll or two sit on the garden bench beside Hope Ruby.

However, before I designed Lovie's Garden that would have an Enchanted Wood where I included a winding garden path with a small bridge where the imaginary troll could live, a bird bath, and few benches in small secluded places around the garden, I also wanted to have a red brick potager where tulips reached for the blue, spring skies. When the tulips had gone the other way, then corn, tomatoes, okra, and yellow crookneck summer squash could be planted within view of clay pots full of green onions that would hang on the picket fence.

After the Enchanted Wood area was finished, I installed a bluebird house, a bird feeder, and a pergola for Cinderella Fairy Tale pink climbing roses, that also became a trellis for purple and lavender clematis to climb. A large fountain was to sit centered in the middle of the potager for an herb garden which could also grow mustard greens.

Before the garden came to life, I would buy several peony plants with the bright idea of planting them in my daughter's backyard until I moved to my new location and had the hardscape completed to be ready for the first plants. Of course, peonies would be the first plants in the ground.

"Here's the plan," I said to Peyton. "I'm buying several peony plants. I'll plant the peonies at your house. When I get the bones of my new garden laid out and installed, we'll dig up the peonies and plant them in my garden. Then divide them after three years so you can have half of the plants for the new home you and Chris are building. One thing though, we have that trip planned to Babyland General Hospital in Helen, Georgia where the Cabbage Patch Kids are born. You'll have to get your hubs to water the plants while we're out of town with the girls. The heat is already getting unbearable and he can't let the newly-planted peonies die. Do you think Chris will remember to keep them watered until we get back? I know he doesn't mind cooking, cleaning, and golfing, but will he stand outside and deep water plants in this heat?"

Peyton said, "I'll call and remind him while we're away. He'll do it."

I planted two different colors of pinks—pale pink and medium pink herbaceous peonies, one yellow Itoh peony which is more like a tree peony that has woody stems and doesn't need to be staked, and one medium pink tree peony that I put in the back of the Kids' Corner area of the garden. About six plants total. Then I lightly mulched them before we left on our girls' trip.

Once Peyton and I were settled in with the girls in a Georgia hotel, Peyton called Chris to check in. After the girls talked to their daddy on speaker phone Peyton chimed in, "Hey, what did you do today?" Chris said, "I worked half a day and then worked in some golf."

"Did you remember to water the peonies? Mom's got a small fortune tied up in those peonies. You can't let them die."

"I watered the peonies. The peonies will be fine. What did ya'll do today?"

"Tried to get Hayden's chewing gum out of the carpet in the back of the car. She chewed through the entire pack of gum Mom gave her during that nasty rain storm we were caught in while driving windy mountain roads."

"Sounds fun. She just spit the gum out and threw it on the floorboard on the carpet?"

"Yep."

"I guess you were glad Harper's not old enough to chew yet. Did you get the gum out?"

"No. Ahhh, it's going to take some work. Might need a little elbow grease. Maybe you'll have better luck."

"Mmm-hmm. Nice."

"Love you. I'll check in tomorrow.—Don't forget to water the peonies!"

The next phone call home went something like this: "Hey, we're in Helen. Did you water the peonies today?"

"Yeeeeeesss, I watered the *peonies* today. I'm *not* forgetting to water the peonies. What have you guys been up to?"

"We took the girls to Babyland General so they could get their Cabbage Patch Kids out of the hospital. Then Mom had the bright idea of putting baby Hope in a crib full of Cabbage Patch babies for a photo shoot and we almost lost her for a minute—she blended in so well with the other babies. They didn't move and she didn't move and all of those big eyes just looking up at us…but we found her when she blinked. And you're sure you watered the peonies?"

"Hmmmph!"

"Okay, okay. Just making sure you don't let those peonies die before we get back. Love you!"

After a few more similar phone calls and peony reminders, I said, "Honey, you might want to let up on the peony watering reminders. I'm afraid Chris might take a blow torch to the peony bushes." Laughing, I added, "I'd hate to lose that yellow Itoh and pink tree peony—and all the others!"

Once we made it back home with the Cabbage Patch babies and the real baby dolls, and once Lovie's Garden hardscape preparation was finished by strong capable hands, I was able to move the peonies into their new home. More digging. In my experience, digging up a plant always seems harder than digging a hole and planting a new plant.

When it came time to put rose bushes in place, I dug 29 holes and called Peyton. "Help! I need you to come over and dig 11 more holes. I am bushed! And so sick of looking at a shovel."

I then added the pink tree peony with future satiny pink blooms that would be spectacular saucer-plate size in the Kids Corner behind the concrete bench near the Mr. Puss n' Boots statue that guarded that section of the garden.

Later, when my mailbox filled up with flower catalogs every spring with at least 41 different types of peony cultivars, I fell in love with other peony varieties. I wanted them all. Festiva Maxima, a white peony with a drizzle of red in the center, became my next obsession. The next year, I added a couple of coral varieties I'd previously promised myself I wouldn't fall in love with. Oh, treacherous heart. I couldn't resist being charmed by "Coral Charm" and "Coral Sunset."

One oddity—the yellow peony turned out to be an Itoh peony that was an incredible champagne color with ruby streaks in the center. The plant is always loaded with big fat blooms and is the second peony to bloom every year, right after the pink tree peony Mr. Puss n' Boots guards. Who knows, this might be the year to add another peony variety—a true yellow.

With all of these different peony colors to choose from for the Peony Tea Parties, I could either use the same color of peony blooms, or mix the pinks and whites and place the centerpiece on a tablecloth that helped enhance the flowers and make the blooms dazzle while surrounded with teatime goodies.

But what if spring thunderstorms ruin the peonies, a reader might ask. Well then, I have been known to throw a Dahlia Dahling Party in summertime when the 10-inch dinner plate dahlias are blooming. A girl must be able to not only have her cake and cookies, she must be able to eat them too!

On a last note, when Peyton, Chris, and the girls moved into their new home and it came time to plant more peonies in their backyard I said to Peyton, "Are we ready to dig up our peonies and divide them so you can put your share in your garden?"

She laughed and said, "No way. I'll buy my own peonies so I only have to dig one hole for each plant instead of digging, dividing, and replanting. And by the way, once I get them planted we'll be going on vacation so can you come water my peonies?"

I chuckled. "I sure will Babe, and you won't even have to call me every day to remind me—I'll bet Chris is so glad he's going with you on *this* trip so he doesn't have to be reminded to water the peonies!"

∽ 2 ∾
Roach Coach Angel

Since I couldn't find anyone else interested in riding horses at the Gleneagles Equestrian center in Scotland, I traveled alone to Great Britain and scheduled my itinerary like a general planning on conquering a continent.

I knew what plays I wanted to see in London, and bought tickets for three consecutive nights. I'd been wanting to see *Les Misérables* at Queen's Theatre for eons. Visiting the world's most magnificent show would be such a treat. I was not disappointed—until after the performance was over and it was time to leave.

Everyone rushed to the black cabs that looked like enormous roaches. I'd been told to hail one of those cabs instead of other cabs that were off limits because some drivers weren't licensed cab drivers and broke city rules depriving London of revenue.

Now, there were no cabs, and no people. Feeling uncomfortable, alone, and *une femme misérable* myself, I began walking to another street until I spotted a black cab and hailed it to take me back to my hotel.

The next night, after a different play, I experienced the same scenario. Except this time, the night was darker, the area of town more ominous. At least I wasn't standing alone. A middle-aged woman and her elderly mother stood nearby. I approached them and asked if they would like to share a cab if one should appear.

A cab did appear, but it wasn't a black cab. It was blue. We didn't want to take a chance on being left stranded so I negotiated a price to our different hotels and we hopped in. My new friends were dropped off and once alone with the cab driver and feeling comfortable he wasn't going to rob me and then dispose of my body in the Thames River, I asked him if I could count on him to pick me up the next night and told him which play I'd be attending and the location. He assured me he'd be in the cab lineup waiting exclusively for me. I breathed easier and prayed God would, indeed, provide me transportation so the next night I wouldn't have to stand by myself— stranded once again.

So, the next evening, I exited the theatre with the push of a pulsing crowd. My cab driver, with his blue bomb, was nowhere around. Nor were any other cabs. Perhaps the theatre had let out a little early.

And then I saw it. A black cab sitting at a distance away from the theatre. One lone roach coach. I prayed as I made power-walk strides toward the cab, trying to keep from running to avoid drawing attention my way. "Lord, please, let that be my black cab! Please God, oh please God, let me get there first!"

Then the crowd moved like a raging sea in the direction of the roach chariot that had my name on it. And they began to run. As they ran, so did I. We were off! But I had a head, belly, and elbow start. As I ran, I kept praying bullet prayers. "Help me beat them Lord! Make these legs run faster than theirs."

And when the crowd saw I was sprinting hard for the last stretch and would beat them by a long shot, they gave up and melted back into the shadows of the heat-oppressed night. Opening the door, I gasped, "Can you please...take me to...uh...Knightsbridge...uh...Sloane Street...uh...let me get my breath...uh! *Ummmm, where am I staying?* Yes! The Cadogan Hotel!"

My cab driver looked amused and nodded. Unlike the cab drivers of the previous nights, he never said a word. I pondered all that had happened back at the theatre. How could those people not have seen my cab as soon as I had? And why hadn't the driver moved his cab forward when he saw the theatre-goers pouring from the doors? I pinched myself to make sure I wasn't living in the Twilight Zone.

We rode in silence. I was too amazed to speak. When we reached the Cadogan Hotel, I leaned forward and handed the driver several pound notes and asked if the amount was enough. His lips curved into an amused smile, as if he knew a secret. Nodding again, he accepted the amount along with the tip. When I stepped out of the cab, the now familiar Cadogan Hotel doorman held open the door to greet me as usual.

"Good evening, madam. Did you have a pleasant evening at the theatre?"

I replied, "I enjoyed the play very much. However...."

Turning around, I wanted to get another glimpse of my roach coach and the mysterious driver. But he was gone. He couldn't have driven off that quickly without my seeing at least the car's tail lights.

"As you were saying madam?"

"Yes, I enjoyed the play. And I think…." But here I stopped. Who would believe that God heard my prayer and sent an angel to pick me up at the theatre and drive me to my hotel?

In my room, I prayed, thanking God for blessing me with His provision and care. During the rest of my trip, I prayed about every mode of transportation including trains, planes, and roach coaches. And after returning to the States, I never stopped praying without ceasing about every little thing.

Once upon a time, Cinderella needed transportation. A godmother turned a pumpkin into a coach and a mouse into a footman.

Once upon a scary night, I needed safe transportation, and my Father provided a roach coach and an angel driver.

Cinderella's was a fairy tale.

Mine was a miracle.

❧ 3 ❧
Two Old Women

Unto him that is able to do exceeding abundantly above all that we ask or think, according to the power that worketh in us....
Ephesians 3:20

Deep in the heart of Alaska, a man was mauled by a grizzly. Though I wasn't there during this violent attack, or even know him personally, I did know a friend of his through Facebook. Stunned when Irene posted this accident on her Facebook wall, I visualized her friend's attack, and it was difficult to get "the movie" of this ordeal out of my mind. I felt a kinship during his hours of need. For we are kindred spirits.

Then later, back to my own life as usual, I had one of those days where everything that could go wrong went wrong. Nothing like a grizzly attack, but I experienced Murphy's law to the nth degree. An entire list of tasks and chores was piling up and the stress was almost unbearable. Farm equipment had broken down. My car had rebelled because a rodent was hiding dog food in a strategic location beneath the hood. Squirrels had found the T.V. cable wire more tempting than walnuts. My to-do list needed immediate attention. I couldn't find a document I needed. All was in chaos. I began to pace the floor of my dining room, calling out to God, "Help me God! Help me find the document I need and have been searching for!"

Even more exasperated when I didn't get an answer, I continued pacing the floor and praying. "Okay then God, I need a certain book my daughter read when she was in school. I also read it and she was right about it being a phenomenal book. It was about two old Eskimo women who no longer pulled their own weight so tribal members had to wait on them for their needs. They were no longer useful to the tribe so during an exceptionally harsh winter they'd been left at the old camp to die while the others moved on searching for food and wild game. I can't remember the name of the book, God. But, those two old women decided they wanted to live and found a way to survive by using their wisdom and lifetime skills. It was the most encouraging and motivational book about survival and forgiveness I think I've ever read. I need that book for such a time as this but I can't even remember the name of it! Lord, help me find that book about the two old Alaskan women. Help me remember the book's title—refresh my memory so I can buy it. Read it. And gain courage from the story. And I need it *now* God!"

Nothing like bossing God around. I waited expectantly, but there was no remembrance. No jogging of gray matter. My brain had turned to mush. All I heard was a tree frog and cicada orchestra tuning up outside, and since they were speaking in foreign tongues, I couldn't understand a single word they said. Where was my counselor and my comforter when I needed Him? Where was my intercessor?

"Oh God," I cried out, "do you even care about the little things?" But deep in my heart, I knew God cared about *everything.* I just didn't understand why some prayers were answered and others weren't. But I was not to know the mind of God. My job was to have faith and to trust.

Such a difficult job sometimes.

A couple of days later, I drove to the Post Office to pick up my mail. There in the box was a package from Fairbanks, Alaska. Who did I know in Alaska? No one. So I was surprised when I recognized the name on the return address as being the same as my Facebook friend—Irene. The same Irene who had the friend who'd been mauled by the grizzly. I'd never met her personally, only through cyberspace.

I thought back to when I had first joined Facebook, not something I particularly wanted to do because of all of the crazies out there trying to scam people. However, it was a way to stay connected and meet new people so I thought I'd give it a try. Irene was one of the first of my many friends. Her state was quite a distance from the southern state of Tennessee. I'd always wanted to visit Alaska, but in my travels had never journeyed there. So we chit-chatted about the weather and scads of snow, hours of daylight or none, and Irene would "like" things I might write about or photographs I posted. And I in turn "liked" and enjoyed the photographs she posted. They reminded me of a cousin who'd once lived on the Yukon River and the stories he told about buying his first bathtub for a one-room cabin. Before that, he'd *roughed it* by heating water. I recalled the stories about rowdies or criminals being chained to bulldozers until they could be flown out of the wilderness and taken to a town and a real jail.

When Irene became a friend, I especially enjoyed her

postings from the North Country. With such infrequent and casual contact, I was surprised when she notified me in March of 2012 that she was sending me a book. But, I never received the book and thought Irene had forgotten about the promise, so I forgot about the book as well.

Imagine my surprise now, when I opened the package to read the words *Two Old Women* by Velma Wallis, the same book title I'd begged God for a few days earlier. I could not believe my good fortune but immediately gave thanks, astonished at this form of supernatural experience. God didn't give me simply the title, He gave me the physical book, routing it through Irene! I raced home, opened my laptop to log in to Facebook and researched all past correspondence I'd had with my friend. Had either of us mentioned this book before? *Was this for real?* Had she previously mentioned the title of this book and I'd forgotten about it?

What I found was the following: In March, three months earlier, Irene had told me she was going to send me a book. There was no mention of a title. She'd never hinted at the book's contents. Never mentioned story plot. Nothing. Only that I would enjoy it. Our conversation up to that point had never been too personal. I went over our correspondence about her friend who'd been mauled by the grizzly bear. How she'd asked for prayer for him. I read where I'd asked for an address to send him a card of encouragement and I remembered sending it. There was information about the 20 surgeries required to repair her friend's face and destroyed jaw. There was no mention of *Two Old Women*.

What could I surmise?

I'd mysteriously received this book from her at a time when I desperately needed it. It had to be a God thing. I immediately messaged her. "Irene, I received *Two Old Women* in the mail just now and thank you so very much. However, why did you send it? Why that particular book?" She replied, "I'd promised you a book in March but hadn't gotten around to sending it until now. Sorry for my being lazy and not getting to the Post Office to mail it earlier."

When I explained to her what had happened, my having a rough day and crying out to the Lord for this book though I couldn't for the life of me remember the title, Irene was so excited. Thrilled!

Here's her side of our story:

"I read to the children in the schools. Some of the children have so much with all of the latest electronic devices and are always on their cell phones and texting and therefore, are no longer motivated and are losing reading skills. So I read to them from *Two Old Women*. Of course, I leave out some parts not suitable for young children, however, the theme of the book is all about encouragement and motivation. So, I thought you might like a copy."

She was elated when I told her what had happened through my praying a few days earlier for the book—that in June, I'd received what I'd prayed for along with God giving me the desires of my heart. I said, "Feel free to tell your school children about the incident and how awesome God is to answer provision through prayer."

Though Irene had initially forgotten her promise, God is a God who never forgets. He hadn't forgotten Irene's promise, nor had He forgotten my desires, and during my meltdown He had prompted Irene to send Velma's book—at the very moment I had been praying for it, since its arrival was a few days after I asked God for the title so I could make the purchase. God knew before I cried out to Him what I needed. He knew the exact hour of my need and the exact second the book would be in my hands. And He gave me more than a title to a book. He gave me the physical book, and later He showed me where to find the lost document.

His timing is always perfect!

∼ 4 ∽
Delight Comes in Layers

I used to be amazed at the number of Christian writers and bloggers putting their stories out through traditional publishing or by self-publishing books, blogs, or vlogs. When personal computers became affordable, the masses instantly had a "voice" and became writers and speakers. But weren't there enough people preaching and teaching the Gospel? Would it really make a difference to have one more person out there in the world quoting scriptures and conversing about theologians' commentary?

The answer popped into my head immediately: God meets each individual in a different place because each individual was created uniquely. Therefore, various stories and recapped experiences are needed. And since individuals have different interests and varied stories to tell, the more the Gospel is shared along with personal testimonies, the greater the likelihood that one of those stories will register with a nonbeliever or an agnostic who might be riding the fence of their salvation. Another person's testimony could possibly help usher an unbeliever into the throne room of grace.

I may never know how much my testimony has impacted

others or how effective my efforts have been until I get to heaven. But I can hope that once home, God will share the results with me and tell me if my efforts were effective or not, if He was delighted with the fruit of my labor, and if my outreach to others for Him made progress my eyes couldn't see.

I knew this much, God had delighted me with many gifts and "treasured moments" before I ever thought about trying to delight Him in return with the meager and limited resources I own here on earth. And I began thinking about God and a word He'd used: *delight*. Just like my earthly father, when he was alive, loved delighting me—especially during the holidays when celebrating the birthday of Jesus—my heavenly Father loved delighting me more. His gifts, if I was paying attention, were seen as layered delight throughout a lifetime of walking with Him.

Yes, God has always delighted in giving His children good gifts. Matthew 7:11 tells us *if you then, being evil, know how to give good gifts to your children, how much more will your Father who is in heaven give what is good to those who ask Him! In everything, then, do to others as you would have them do to you. For this is the essence of the Law and the prophets.*

These days, my all-time favorite verse about the word *delight* is this: *Delight yourself in the Lord; and He will give you the desires of your heart.* Psalm 37:4

This verse has resonated with me numerous times.

But how could I ever delight the Lord back with a gift of my own when He's the One who created the Universe and owns all the cattle on a thousand hills? How could I possibly give Him any earthly thing that would please Him? Delighting my earthly father was easy in comparison. When Daddy was still with me, all I had to do to please him was to prepare his favorite dessert, Four Layer Delight, and he was happy for days.

But what to give my heavenly Father—the God who has everything—to delight Him? There was and still is one recipe: I was to give Him *all* of me, just as He gave His One and Only Son for the entire world. Through the gift of His Son, I was assured of redemption and the way back to Him for eternal life. It was as hard and as simple as that, once the life-changing steps were taken.

Once the messiness of surrendering all has been laid out, wrapped up, and tied with a bow, other ways to delight God will come—the fruit of labor in His service will be produced as a sweet sacrifice—though one can never outdo God in gift giving or in trying to delight Him. He has always been and will always be the best gift giver ever, showering His children throughout a lifetime of love layers embedded with delightful gifts. Even during the hard times sure to come.

I've shared the recipe with the ingredients to make my heavenly Father happy, now I'll share the ingredients to a recipe that made my earthly father happy until time for him to leave this world and return home. I hope it delights your loved ones as much as it does mine.

Four Layer Delight

Ingredients

    1 stick softened butter or margarine
    1 cup flour
    ½ cup chopped pecan nuts
    8 ounces softened cream cheese
    1 large carton of Cool Whip
    1 cup sifted powdered Confectioner's sugar
    2 packages instant chocolate pudding and pie mix
    3 cups milk

Preparation

1st layer: Mix one softened stick of butter or margarine, 1 cup of flour, and ½ cup chopped pecan nuts. Spread in a square pan and bake for 10 minutes at 350° F. (An 8 x 8 inch Pyrex dish is good. If you use the 9 x 13 size, double the recipe.)

2nd layer: Cream 8 oz. softened cream cheese. Add 1 cup of Cool Whip from large carton + 1 Tablespoon of milk and 1 cup sifted powdered sugar. Mix together and spread over first layer.

3rd layer: Mix two packages of instant chocolate pudding and pie mix with three cups of milk. Pour over other layers.

4th layer: Spread remaining Cool Whip over the pudding. Garnish with toasted pecans on top if so desired.

❧ 5 ❧
Keep It Moist

At one time in my life, I had a sweet tooth for carrot cake with cream cheese icing. Since one wasn't going to fall out of the sky, I was going to have to make my own. In my 20s and not that great a cook—gravy was a mystery and biscuits were a lardy challenge back in the day when my biscuits had some lightweight fluffy heft to them.

I did know how to do one thing with relish, and that was bake cakes.

When I was 12 years old and needing some extra cash, I used to bake cakes for my mother's friends' dinner parties. They loved my cakes. Those ladies enjoyed singing my praises and always asked my mother how I managed to always bake such a moist cake. "However does she do it? Could you ask that little darlin' for us?"

"The trick," I shared with Mother, "is to undercook the cakes five minutes. But don't reveal the secret of my success." Of course Mother let the cake out of the bag. But the orders still kept pouring in.

Since I was a cake-baking prodigy at 12, how hard would a carrot cake be at 20-something?

I found a trusted cookbook and combed the pages, looking for a beaut of a carrot cake. Found one!

I measured. Broke eggs. Stirred. Blended. Dumping in the rest of the ingredients, I wondered about this recipe that would have me grate orange peels to throw into the mix. Hmmmm. It would be an interesting carrot cake with that bright colored orangy zest from a citrus fruit. But one I couldn't wait to sink my teeth into. I was creating what looked to be the most magnificent carrot cake ever baked on planet earth.

Sticking the pans into the oven, I began working on the cream cheese icing. Once the cake had cooled, I swirled the thick icing between layers, on top, and around the sides. No naked cakes for me or my family and friends—lots of icing it would be. I was a "shower me with sugar" kind of gal.

And then the first bite. *Wait a minute! This tastes nothing like carrot cake. This. Is. Something. Else. Wait a minute. I never grated carrots to put in the cake. Wait a minute. That's because the recipe never called for carrots! How can a carrot cake not have carrots in it? Arggghhh!*

Yanking the cookbook back down to take a closer look, I turned to the photo of the beautiful carrot cake, ran my index finger across the page opposite with the recipe, and there it was. In huge letters at the top of the recipe's directions: Williamsburg Orange Cake.

This was no carrot cake! I'd spent all that time making that cake from scratch, to only have my taste buds shiver from culinary shock because what I put in my mouth tasted nothing like carrot cake!

Disappointed to the nth degree, at least I was able to laugh at my mistake. For maybe two seconds. Long enough to grab my car keys to run out and buy me a piece of carrot cake…

which was never moist enough to even come close to one of my cakes. If I'd only chosen the correct recipe.

Later, after the desire for carrot cake had faded, I discovered the Williamsburg Orange Cake was incredible. So instead of sharing a carrot cake recipe, I'm sharing the Williamsburg Orange Cake recipe by Oxmoor House—which is also simply divine. Don't forget to shave off five minutes of cooking time and just note that the recipe calls for butter, instead of cream cheese, to be used to make the icing. (You can substitute a cream cheese icing if you prefer.)

Now, I've given away my baking secret. Keep it moist!

(And read directions carefully. A bell should go off in your brain when grating orange zest. There might be a similarity in color between orange zest and carrot gratings, but all similarities end once the first bite goes past the lips!)

Williamsburg Orange Cake

Ingredients

2½ cups all-purpose flour

1½ cups sugar

1½ teaspoons baking soda

¼ teaspoon salt

1½ cups buttermilk

½ cup butter or margarine, softened

¼ cup shortening

3 eggs

1½ teaspoons vanilla extract

1 tablespoon grated orange peel (zest)

1 cup golden raisins, chopped

½ cup finely chopped pecans

Orange peel and sections

Preparation

Combine first 10 ingredients. Blend with an electric mixer 30 seconds on low speed; beat 3 minutes on high speed. Stir in raisins and pecans.

Pour into 3 greased and floured 8-inch round cake pans. Bake at 350° for 30 to 35 minutes or until a wooden pick inserted in center comes out clean. Cool in pans 10 minutes; remove from pans, and cool completely. Spread Williamsburg Butter Frosting between layers and on top and sides of cake. Garnish cake with orange peel and sections.

Williamsburg Butter Frosting

Ingredients

½ cup butter or margarine, softened
4½ cups sifted powdered sugar
1 tablespoon grated orange peel (zest)
4 to 5 tablespoons orange juice

Preparation

Cream butter; gradually add sugar, beating well. Add orange zest and juice; beat until smooth.

~ 6 ~
Turning the Knob for Billy

When I was a young girl and my mother turned the knob of our television—there were no remote controls back then—to search for the latest Billy Graham revival, I must admit I left the room moaning and sighing when I heard Billy preaching. "Really? I was into my show! Do we have to watch this man shouting at people?"

I never thought of Mother as a highly religious person though she curled my hair every Saturday night and dressed me fashionably for church every Sunday, which included black patent Mary Janes, white gloves, and a red rose bud from the front porch trellis on Easter mornings.

Yet, though Mother was diligent in making sure her little chickadee was afforded the opportunity to hear "Just as I Am" and "I Surrender All" sung at the end of a sermon on a regular basis, the Bible was rarely discussed at home when I was growing up. Therefore, I couldn't understand what Mother saw in Billy Graham. Evidently, her quiet faith was a lot like Queen Elizabeth II's—another who favored the fiery sermons of Graham.

Not only was Billy's preaching too loud, so were his ties

and argyle socks. They shouted the Gospel even louder with him from sawdust trails during tent revivals and also from on the stages constructed in humongous stadiums. So why would anyone join the masses to go sit through one of his fiery harangues to be told they were "wicked and sinners all?"

Since his preaching style was not appreciated by me, and his sermons were not the type I could sit through, I retreated to my bedroom and played with Barbie dolls or continued reading *Black Beauty*. Before becoming a mature Christian, there was no way I could comprehend the draw to this North Carolinian's enormous revivals. Even Billy's wife, Ruth Graham was quoted as saying her husband's delivery was too loud. Amen sister!

Not until many years later did a friend share about her experience at The Cove—a retreat built by Graham to bring people together in the mountain wilderness near Asheville, North Carolina to learn more about God from visiting Bible teachers and evangelists. With the friend's revelation, and during an especially dark night of the soul after Mother's passing, I immediately knew it was time for me to take a closer look at Billy Graham.

"If I book a trip to The Cove will you go with me?" I asked this friend.

"Of course, I'd love to go back!"

Off we drove. The profound experience blew us both away. Not only was the mountain air crisp and invigorating, the fall mountain foliage dazzled along with the excellent teaching provided by Jill and Stuart Briscoe. If all of the previously mentioned wasn't enough, the dining room smelled divine and provided lots and lots of ice cream with a nonstop cappuccino and hot chocolate machine offering coffees and hot chocolaty treats to enjoy by the huge fireplace or outside on the veranda while relaxing in one of the comfy rocking chairs.

At the end of the journey, I prayed in the Billy Graham chapel that housed a museum downstairs, and I was totally intrigued and ready to learn all I could about this fiery preacher. When I returned home, I borrowed my pastor's copy of Billy Graham's autobiography. The tome was thick, heavy, unyielding in more ways than one, and could be used as a deterrent against would-be house thieves and recalcitrant demons. How would I ever manage to get through those pages?

But read those pages I did in between getting children to school, mucking out horse stalls, and applying flea prevention ointments to my wandering dogs and cats. Soon I was even more impressed with the man and his words; his personal convictions jumped to the fore. What would become known as the "the Billy Graham rule"—a personal rule that he would not meet alone with another woman, convinced me this North Carolinian was a man of integrity. A man determined to carry out his mission for God, letting nothing stop him from spreading the Gospel and helping save as many of the wicked sinners as he could reach, but also helping to bolster Christians who needed an encouraging message during difficult times.

From Graham's autobiography, I not only learned about the man, his life, and his incredible journey, I was also introduced to a couple of mentors Billy cherished—Henrietta Mears and Billy Sunday. Both stood out for me as well, and their Christian walks were stellar. Henrietta's book, *Dream*

Big, is still one I keep close at hand and reread every year or two for motivation, along with Billy Graham's book on angels, *Angels: God's Secret Agents*. If I hadn't met Billy Graham through his own words, I wouldn't have been introduced to a score of other incredible men and women he knew who also loved God and His Only Son and were willing to spend a life of servitude spreading the message about salvation and eternal life—all in the name of Jesus.

So, I owe a thank you to the man named Billy Graham, but a special thanks goes to Mother—a humble woman of quiet faith who loved hymns like, "Just as I Am," and didn't hesitate to turn the knob for Billy so her child could surrender all.

❧ 7 ❦

Give Me the Exclusive

Once upon a time in my life, just once, instead of asking for The Basic pedicure, I asked for The Exclusive. The total tootsie. And no, not the one where they bring in the fish to eat the dead skin from piglets. Just the fabulous "The Exclusive."

I'd injured my foot and thought my feet needed some extra tender loving care (TLC). Previously, when I splurged for one I'd always gotten the basic pedicure as I was always cognizant of being a good steward of God's money, But this time, my poor foot deserved the best of the best. I wanted the warm soak, the softening exfoliation, the sugar scrub, (Yes, bring on some sugar!) and to be essential-oiled-up. The slough lotion and body butter might be a plus as well, and sounded kind of bold and venturesome.

And boy-howdy, from the moment I made that executive decision, was I in for a tantalizing treat!

When Spring—don't you love her name—opened up a packet of what I call magical crystals and poured them into the water of the pedicure basin, the warm water gradually turned into something difficult for me to describe. It's unlike me to be at a loss for words. At first, my feet felt like they were in a warm pot of Cream of Wheat. Moving my tired and calloused puppy dogs around, I wondered what in the world was going on. But when the Cream of Wheat turned into something that felt like warm Jell-o, and was the consistency of *cold* Jell-o—one giant squid pillow caressing my feet—I thought *this is what living in heaven must be like.*

As I sat there with massaging rollers working out the tension in my back and neck, I must admit I was a tad surprised to be goosed from beneath. The chair actually massaged—yep, the entire body including hind-quarter-ham hocks. It took a few seconds to get over that little shock. Then, with my feet feeling like they were being caressed by this Cream of Wheat/squid-like substance—I'm just going to call it miracle moosh (yeah, I just made that word up for lack of a word to describe what was surrounding my toes and poshing on my piggies)—for the first time in a long while, my feet played and pedicure-bowl happy danced like a child splashing around in an April shower puddle.

Then came the scrub mask. Ahhhh. My calves felt like they'd been let out of their stalls to kick up their heels in spring sunshine. Next came the smooth mud mask. (Now I understood more about frog habitats and why frogs claim mud as their happy place.) Then hot towels. Mega ahhhh. Then the hot rocks massage. I was mega chilling by this time. Then when I thought it couldn't get any better, came more hot towel bliss. The only pedicure that could have topped this experience would have been if I'd also been handed a BLT and a Dr. Pepper over ice with a slice of lime.

Needless to say, I wanted to stay there with Spring's capable hands massaging the hurt away from my foot forever. This event had to be what it must have felt like when Jesus—

the ultimate and ubiquitous healer—washed the feet of others and touched them in such miraculous ways to massage their hurt away forever. The selfless act of foot washing for another is more than a job skill; it's a truly tender loving moment.

I decided the people who wash feet today are special people. I mean, who wants to touch other people's toe jam? There has to be a special place in heaven for foot washers!

I've described all of the above euphoria to now switch gears for a new revelation: The Exclusive pedicure is similar to describing what it's like to study the Bible inductively.

And no, I'm not kidding about this comparison.

There was a time when all of the cross-references in the Bible were daunting and almost annoyed me. So many! And slap dab down the middle of the pages. Just staring back so a reader has to see them.

Constantly nagging, look at me, look at me!

I didn't have time for all of that. Who had time to look up every single verse? There were diapers to be changed. Horse stalls to be mucked. Harness and saddles to be oiled. Room mother duties. Dogs to be bathed after they'd tried to play with live skunks. Rabbits that needed to be fed and caressed after coyote scares. Cats whose ears needed a cleaning and a scratch. Deworming for everybody! (Okay, I'm embellishing. I've never dewormed a rabbit but it has crossed my mind.) Apple trees to be sprayed to keep the worms out. Flowers that needed to be deadheaded. Weeds that needed to be pulled. Clothes to be washed. Elderly parents to get to the doctor. Recitals to be heard. Pastures to be bush hogged.

Ballet performances, tennis, volleyball, and soccer

matches needed support. Fundraisers needed volunteers. Children's Sunday school and Wednesday night classes needed to be taught. Clothes needed mending. And work that had to be done for me to receive a paycheck so groceries could be bought.

My "to do" lists birthed triplets on a daily basis as I methodically ticked off tasks completed and chewed my bottom lip over tasks not done, all while wondering how in the world I would have time to work on my poor callused feet. Trimming toenails—who had time for that when horses and kids needed their hooves and toenails trimmed?

I had no extra time. Period.

Until the King of Kings began wooing me. I'd known Him since I was a young girl. But then He began to *wonderfully* woo. He courted me with a surprising gentleness that sparked my thirsty curiosity. His Holy Spirit began to caress, gently enshrouding me with His love like a warm blanket fresh out of the dryer. Like a puppy or child on wash day, I fell into a pile of warm-blanket-love and wiggled every time He opened the door and revealed to me something new about His character. This warm-blanket-love, however, came with a peace that passes all understanding.

And after those blanket hugs, *woe is me.* I felt that Jesus wanted me to know more about Him so I could better share with others—adults as well as children—just how awesome He is. Just how wide, high, and deep is the love of the Only Begotten Son of God. I knew pretty much the high and wide, yet Jesus wanted me knowing *the deep*. And while exploring the depths of the man who is also God, I fell not just in love, but totally head-over-heels. But how to know this lover more intimately?

Walking out on a limb for Him wasn't an easy thing for me to do. Christians don't always agree with one another about what the Bible says. And addressing nonbelievers? My knees knocked at the thought of the sometimes viciousness of those who claim to be agnostics and atheists. I was good at deworming animals, but deworming people of their false beliefs or no belief at all? Yikes! There had to be someone more experienced that God could use for this job. I had enough ear scratching, barn mucking, and fill-in-the-blank-and-I-did-it "to do" on my platter.

Yet, I couldn't resist those loving moments I'd experienced with the One who could woo like no other lover. So I began combing through His words, page after thin page of a Greek-Hebrew Bible and several other translations. I wanted to know everything there was to know. I couldn't gulp the truth in fast enough. Verses I'd read my entire life jumped to life on the page. Scripture was illuminated. There was more than commandments to learn. More than "Jesus loves me this I know" and "Zacchaeus was a wee little man." There were blood covenants. Promises. Wars and rumors of war. Forgivable sin. Unforgivable sin. Love affairs gone bad. Unfulfilled prophecies. Along with the icing on this humdinger of a cake was pure, unadulterated, redeeming love.

Using the cross references and other study tools to better understand Him, I began studying the Bible inductively. Through the more in depth understanding of His Word, not only did my feet happy dance as though they were in warm miracle moosh anticipating an incredible massage, my entire mind, body, and soul happy danced. Forevermore I would be saying, "Let me check cross references—I don't want The Basic scripture pedi. Give me The Exclusive!"

I'd discovered there was even more—if that could be possible—to this "Everlasting Love" because my entire cerebral mass had been massaged with a mind blowing brain-i-cure by the hot Rock of all time—Jesus Christ—as my personal, The Exclusive, masseuse who massages more than piggies or tootsies. He massages the entire person: Body, soul, mind, and spirit.

Now this—the discovery of inductive Bible study for a total brain-i-cure instead of simply a total tootsie pedicure—was TLC to infinity. What an everlasting and loving moment when I knew to say, "Bring on the good stuff. Give me The Exclusive!"

Sanctify the Lord God in your hearts: and be ready always to give an answer to every man that asketh you a reason of the hope that is in you with meekness and fear: Having a good conscience; that, whereas they speak evil of you, as of evildoers, they may be ashamed that falsely accuse your good conversation in Christ. 1 Peter 3:15-16

❧ 8 ॐ
I Am My Beloved's and My Beloved Is Mine

I must be honest. There have been times I've had trouble praying. Times when I was exhausted simply thinking about praying. Was God even listening? There have been times when prayers weren't answered. I saw no visible results. Some call those times the "dark night of the soul." But I know my Adonai hears every prayer and that even during the dry times that turn into cry times, and when prayer time is elusive, my Lord is with me.

During one of these silent times, I read scripture that made me wince. Revelation 2:4: *"I have somewhat against thee, because thou hast left thy first love."* And I felt guilty for not spending enough time in my prayer closet, because I know prayer is my direct line of communication to the Father and His Son and I know that the Lord loves me.

As the children's song goes, "...for the Bible tells me so."

I wasn't spending enough time with Him. I had forsaken my first love, though He had not forsaken me. Could He possibly miss me? So I decided to purchase a band of silver to wear as an everyday reminder of the romantic words in Song of Solomon 6:3: *I am my beloved's, and my beloved is mine.* The embossed words were crafted in Hebrew (אני לדודי ודודי לי) and I touched them often during the day with my thumb.

Yet, I have another confession: I haven't always been so infatuated with the words from Solomon's song. When I was a teen, I thought the lovers a tad cheesy. Hilarious even. The words formed meaning I obviously didn't totally understand.

I'd thought it pretty funny that the "lover" in that book had described his darling in this manner: I liken you, my darling, to a mare harnessed to one of the chariots of Pharaoh. Bwah-ha-ha-ha-ha-ha had been my teen response. The horses I'd been riding were beautiful to me, but long in the face, long in the tooth, and had large flaring nostrils. Having a boyfriend calling out, "Hey, horse face!" might get a guy clocked with a barn bucket or a bale of hay.

And then there was "darling" describing herself in 2:1: *I am the rose of Sharon...*. The Rose of Sharon trees I was familiar with that grew in the southern United States were called "trash trees" by some because they grow anywhere and have sucker roots running all over the place that have to be kept in check so they won't take over the entire yard. What a nuisance! My grandmother, Mary Kate, loved her Rose of Sharon trees that bloomed most of the summer. Yet when my mother planted some near the back deck of her mountaintop home, I thought, *Why is she planting trash trees? They're like mint. High maintenance unless root bound.*

A few years later, after my "trash tree" and "Hey, horse face!" musings had been long since shelved in the back of my mind, the Lipizzan horse show came to town. These horses that had been trained the same way as those in the Spanish

Riding School of Vienna, Austria weren't the same as stocky-chested quarter horses used for barrel racing, bull dogging, or bronc riding. Even though quarter horses, warmbloods, and thoroughbreds were beautiful to me, they didn't compare to the Lipizzans who were trained and schooled in the art of the dance. Classical dressage.

There they were softly thundering through the arena with orchestrated moves that enhanced powerful and sleek, supple bodies. Poetry in motion pranced before me as the horses performed the half-pass, counter-canter, flying change, pirouette, passage, and piaffe before demonstrating the "airs above the ground," highly controlled stylized jumps, and other movements called the levade, the courbette, the capriole, the croupade and the ballotade.

The beautiful stallions I beheld took my breath away. I was totally smitten. With perfect white bodies (technically they're called gray—gray skin but with white hair after reaching maturity) they obeyed every command. With large and expressive eyes, the Lipizzaners were the most beautiful equines I'd ever seen.

Graceful and gorgeous were perfect words to describe them as they demonstrated haute école or "high school" movements.

I fell head over heels in love with the muscular breed that was developed in Slovenia. I could picture teams of Lipizzans harnessed to one of the chariots of Pharaoh, prancing in place while waiting for the one lucky enough to gather up their reins. I imagined myself riding one of those handsome beauties, becoming one with the equine, my legs squeezing the horse's sides for the cue to move forward into a gallop to race with the wind alongside crashing waves.

One day after the Lipizzan performance, I sat with my parents on their back deck, enjoying the antics of the hummingbirds that hovered near the Rose of Sharon blossoms, thirsty for a drink of succulent nectar. Mother had planted different varieties of the small trees and they blessed us with white, pink, and lavender blossoms. I'd never really taken the time to closely examine their flowers until then—totally relaxed with a glass of lemonade on a warm summer's day— and it was as though I recognized their true beauty for the first time, appreciating their loveliness. Resplendent in all their glory, the nectar-filled blooms tempted the hummingbirds with their sweet love offering. And I recalled Beloved in Song of Solomon referring to herself: *I am a rose of Sharon....* So, Beloved was stunning.

It was then that the descriptions in Song of Solomon made sense to me. By that time, I'd done some research on the horses in King Solomon's day by studying paintings in college Art History. The kings and pharaohs bred horses not only for strength and stamina, but also for beauty. The horses were kept in top shape—exercised daily—should they be needed for battle. I realized that comparing Beloved to a mare harnessed to one of the chariots of Pharaoh was more than a compliment, the comparison reeked of romance. Simply touching the soft velvety nose of a horse and having them nudge or caress one back is an act of love in itself and can lift a weary soul.

Beloved comparing herself to a rose of Sharon, was also immensely romantic. Even if the rose of Sharon in Israel was different from the Rose of Sharon in the southern United States, a rose is a rose and ornately delicate and exquisite.

For Beloved to say, "My lover *is* mine and I *am* his," well, it just doesn't get any more romantic than that, especially with the lover replying, "How beautiful you are, my darling! Oh, how beautiful!"

After that summer day's revelation, every time I now rub my thumb over the raised Hebrew letters of my silver band that spell out "I *am* my beloved's and *my* beloved is mine," I'm reminded how much God loves me. How much His Son loves me. How the Holy Spirit loves me enough to live inside me to be my Comforter and Counselor. That Jesus is my first love, the one who loves me so much He laid down His life for me.

I don't even have to share the intimacies of my mind, heart and spirit with Him. He already knows everything about me, even the number of hairs on my head. Because He is simply the lover of my soul. He knows. And will always love me eternally—forever and amen.

It doesn't get any more romantic than that.

"Come unto me, all ye that labour and are heavy laden, and I will give you rest." Matthew 11:28

Rend your heart and not your garments, and turn unto the Lord your God; for he is gracious and merciful, slow to anger, and of great kindness, and repenteth him of the evil. Joel 2:13

~ 9 ~
Romance on the River

The date seemed like a dream. Something I'd only read about in romance novels. To be picked up and whisked off to a marina where an easy-on-the-eyes guy would have a boat waiting for a trip upriver to Harrison Bay State Park, Tennessee and an incredible breakfast I'd only heard rumors about, seemed divine.

As the sun continued to climb into the sky, a few fluffy clouds could be spotted against a mostly azure blue. There was a peaceful morning calm upon shimmery water as the boat began to slide across the open expanse to head toward the promise of heaping stacks of syrup-drenched pancakes with sausage on the side.

Upon arriving at our destination 30 minutes later, I spotted the restrooms on the slope above the dock and told my romantic guy I'd be only a minute. The benches outside of the restrooms looked inviting, so the perfect place for my date to wait.

While in the restroom stall, I kept thinking about how much fun I was having—how I hoped I was making a good impression. Yet, while thinking about this romantic date, I noticed the woman's feet in the stall next to me. She had extremely large feet. *Wow...I wonder where she buys her* shoes. *Those aren't piglets at the end of her feet, those are full grown pigs.*

Then I noticed her feet could use a pedi. *Those feet are a tad rough around the edges and in need of a mule hoof rasp, and her toenails could use some shellac or something. If I had that much hair on my toes, I'd wax those pigs. Just sayin'.*

But what I noticed next shocked me down to my Plumb Parfait Pink toenails. *Why are this woman's feet pointed toward the back of the toilet? Maybe her stall has a bidet. Never could figure out how to use those. Oh well, to each her own.*

Dismissing the woman in the stall next to me from my mind, I kept thinking how good the orange juice and coffee were going to taste when I finally ordered my pancakes. *Maybe I should get bacon instead of sausage. But both would be a nice touch. And I haven't had a sausage biscuit slathered with mustard in soooo long. Should I get caffeinated coffee, or decaf? Caffeine makes me chatter more. I'll stick with decaf. Should I eat like a Gone With the Wind bird or would this date appreciate a girl with a hearty appetite? Pancakes, bacon, and sausage, move over baby and make way for some strawberries and cantaloupe too, because here I come!*

Opening the stall door, I stepped over to the mirror and wash basin, washed and dried my hands, then smoothed down windblown hair and checked my makeup. *At least my mascara isn't running. Should I apply more lipstick? Better not. I've kept the romantic one waiting long enough. He probably hears the biscuits and sawmill gravy calling and his stomach probably thinks his throat's been cut. Better hurry.*

When I walked toward the restroom's exit, I was stunned

to see a tall guy standing in the doorway holding the door open. *Why is he doing that? Everybody and their sister's black cat can now see inside the ladies' room!* Totally embarrassed that the man had walked into the women's restroom by mistake—or maybe something worse, perhaps he was a peeping Tom pervert—I averted my gaze and looked down before making an attempt to ease by him, hoping he wasn't planning on kidnapping me. I mentally rehearsed my practiced Karate chop and Judo throw just in case. *Maybe now those self-defense classes I took in college will come in handy.*

Then I saw them.

Oh, No! Those feet. Those sandals. THOSE WHOPPER PIGS! They belong to the person who had been in the stall next to mine. Wait a minute. Jeez-Louise and HOLY COW! I shared the restroom with a...oh...my...goodness, and I declare...a full grown...MAN! And one with hairy pigs at that! Lord, say it ain't so!

The next thing I knew, this full grown man put his arm around me and as we strolled out of the restroom hugged up together like long-lost lovers, he bent down and whispered in my ear, the same ear that had previously been tucked under his armpit, "Honey, I think you used the men's restroom by mistake."

I managed to mumble, "Uh...sorry...." Oh. Big. Fat. NAW! And now this man must have been thinking, *Love these Southern gals from East Tennessee who can't read a lick.*

Imagine my date's surprise when I strolled out of the men's room tucked beneath the armpit of another man. When the stranger and I said our goodbyes—mine was a sheepish gesture—I had to then explain…the other man. My date was kind enough to grin without laughing as I was trying to tell him I wasn't really that man's honey even though we'd just shared…I decided to hush about my embarrassing faux pas before I made matters worse about what we'd just shared.

Let me simply add that I made quite the impression all right. I could hardly eat a bite. So much for breakfast romance on the river.

And if anyone ever repeats this story about me, I'll vow and declare up one side and down the other that they lied.

❧ 10 ☙
A Strange Thing Happened on the Backside of a Boondock Somewhere Near Montgomery

One summer, during a period of my life when I began to hear from God in the most amazing ways—ways that sometimes scared my socks off because previously, I hadn't been used to hearing from Him so clearly—I was driving by myself down I-65 through Alabama to Destin, Florida. My goal was meeting up with my daughter, along with a friend of hers and her friend's parents at their beach home. The plan was to do some bicycling, have lots of reading time while resting beneath an umbrella, maybe jump a wave or two, eat lots of seafood, watch great movies at night, and relax in general while having fun.

While listening to a Christian radio program just north of Montgomery, Alabama I was inspired to pray: "Lord, what would you have me do?"

While I was praying—with my eyes open of course—I saw a sign on the right side of the road that notified travelers of a Confederate Memorial Park up ahead. Suddenly, I felt a strong tug on the heart strings, or in my spirit—what was happening was questionable—to go there. I said, "Well, that's great Lord, but you know I'm expected in Destin. The beach and a book are calling, and I don't have time to go sight-seeing today." The strong feeling to go to the park wouldn't dissipate so I said, "What am I supposed to do there? Can't I visit another time when I'm not on a schedule?"

The answer was a firm, clear, "No"; though I heard nothing audibly, I somehow sensed this reply. The exit ramp loomed ahead and at the last possible moment, I found myself swerving off the interstate to head toward the park. "Okay," I said at the stop sign. "I'll go. But this had better be you, Lord, and would you please tell me what I'm supposed to be doing there? You know I'm a Civil War history buff, but this is not the time to study history. And I really don't have time to traipse through the woods looking at cannons and cannon balls. I'm supposed to be dining on crab boil tonight and I don't want to miss that supper!"

From the interstate, it seemed like I drove forever, the tires lapping up mile after mile. I almost turned around once, thinking I'd lost my ever lovin' mind, but the urgency was still there and I couldn't bring myself to do it, so I kept driving. At last I saw the turn I was to take that would supposedly lead me to the park and my destination. Or, perhaps destiny? Or, God forbid there be a lurking pervert with a knife or gun. Maybe both. Where on earth was I? I prayed I wouldn't have a flat tire because I was on the backside of the boondocks in a heartache-of-a-looking-place. In who-knows-where in a God-forsaken portion of Alabama. My AAA had expired and I didn't know a soul to call if I had car trouble. I began to sense that God was sending me to talk with someone. Yikes! Witnessing to others made me extremely nervous since I had been taught never to talk about religion or politics.

"Are you kidding me? You're sending me into the boonies to talk to someone about Jesus and the Gospel? Don't you have the wrong person for this job? Where's a preacher when you need one?" I had to turn up the air conditioner because I felt a heat wave coming on. I took a deep breath and tried to calm myself because all of my old arguments were, like Martha White self-rising flour, rising. "Okay. I'll try. But you have to help me. You *know* I'm not good at this. No knives. No dodging bullets. *Nothing* scary. And no rabid dogs!"

Not long after I spotted a small church, I soon saw the next turn and drove down another road…and finally I was in the park. As I eased up to a small museum, I noticed only one other automobile in the parking lot. Good. Just one person I was supposed to speak with. I let out a sigh of relief. Until I saw *them*.

Terrified, I sucked in my breath. There, on the other side of the parking lot, an entire family was eating lunch over by some picnic tables. But this wasn't just any family picnic. It was a family reunion! Wait for it…they had a name banner! HUNTINGDON!* Holy cow! Their cars were parked on the other side of the museum parking lot. And there were scads of them. My stomach was queasy now and I thought I'd lose the

Cheetos I'd just eaten. I sat in my car and fought back the urge to tremble.

"Lord, if this is a joke, it's not funny. I am *not* going over there. Those people will have me committed.

"And what would you have me say? 'Oh, hello there. The Lord took me off the interstate several miles and half-a-tank-of-gas-ago to tell you that Jesus is King of Kings and Lord of Lords and Hallelujah, praise be to God, everybody here needs to be SAVED!' Sorry to be so sarcastic Lord, but they will have me institutionalized as sure as the world turns. I'm *not* going over there. I just *can't*."

Hand wringing and ring twisting had commenced. "Being a Christian is too *hard*!"

I looked at my watch and tried to calm down. Late. I was going to be late. The pressing-in-feeling that I was to speak with someone about Jesus wouldn't go away. There was someone in that park I was supposed to speak with.

"Okay. Look, Lord. I can't do it. I'm going to calm down, go in that tiny museum, and since I'm here, look around. Maybe the person is in *there*. Exhorting to hordes is out of my league."

When I entered the museum, there was one person sitting behind the desk. We simultaneously said, "Hello." But then a man and his son stepped through the door behind me. Now there were three people. Who was I supposed to say something to? And what was I supposed to say? "You know God, it would really help if you would fill me in on *The Plan*. Which person? What words? I'm sweating more than Civil War bullets here. Help a girl out."

Nothing. I was hearing absolutely nothing. I looked at my

watch. Time was a-wastin' and so were the waves.

But then, as always, my curiosity got the better of me.

I took in many of the displays. The Confederate Memorial Park wasn't just any Civil War park. This place seemed to be more than a museum. It was a "moving tribute to the men and boys that took up arms in defense of their home state during the Civil War." I discovered that on the site, there was also the Soldiers' Home for Confederate Veterans, and that the 102 acre park included not only the museum, but a research facility, historic structures, ruins, and two cemeteries containing over 300 Confederate soldiers. From 1902 to 1939, the complex had grown to include 22 buildings in addition to the residences. There was a hospital, administration building, mess hall, and a dairy barn and more. I was hooked.

Ninety-one Confederate veterans and 19 widows of veterans lived on this land during its heyday. As the population dwindled, the two cemeteries were filled. It was estimated that as many as 800 residents had lived at the site over the years, and the last surviving veteran living at the home died in 1934. When the complex was closed in 1939, the five remaining veterans' widows were moved to a facility in Montgomery.

There was so much information in this tiny museum I found myself soaking in the history, though I was still anxious about who I was supposed to speak with. Then the man and his son left. Good. Two down. One to go. Perhaps I was supposed to speak with the museum attendant at the desk.

This was all so *questionable.*

Still doubtful, I said, "Okay, Lord, if you're behind this, I'll do it. I'll go chitchat with the attendant and if in conversation she says the word…what word?" I wracked my brain. Then a thought of the little church I had passed on the highway before turning onto the park's road popped into my head. *Church!* Yes! "If she says the word *church*, I'll witness to her if you'll tell me what you want me to say."

Quaking in my sandals I approached the woman, then, had second thoughts. *What if she isn't friendly? Stop it. She works in a museum. It's her job to be friendly. Just go talk with her and get to the bottom of this detour.*

As we began to talk, the attendant telling me about the grounds and Civil War tidbits I asked her about, we had the best chat. A peace fell over me and I enjoyed our conversation. She seemed grateful to be talking with another human being. And I was so grateful to be released from testifying at the "Huntingdon Reunion," I'd totally forgotten I was supposed to *speak* with someone. Then, out of the blue—lo and behold—the woman mentioned the word *church*! I felt like I'd been jolted with a low voltage cattle prod. She'd just said there was a *church* in the park. *That's odd in itself. Okay. I'm on point like a bird dog, Lord. Now what?* But I wasn't being downloaded any information. Then she mentioned *church* again!

I winged it. "You know, I noticed before I got to the park, there's also a little church before the park entrance road."

She began to open up like a lotus blossom about her personal life. "Yes, there are a lot of little churches around here. Why I quit going. People can't get along so churches keep splitting and before you know it there's a new church that's cropped up. I need to get back into church, though. I miss it." A flash of subtle sorrow passed over her beautiful face.

Ahhhhhh. There was my cue. And suddenly, I knew what I was supposed to tell her. "You know, nowadays, you can go online and download Bible studies from the internet." And then the message was so easy-peasy after that. I shared with her about several different Bible studies I'd taught women at my church. Her face lit up the entire room as I shared more, especially about some of the wonderful God-moments I'd had.

Now she was hooked. "I hadn't thought of ordering a Bible study over the internet!" she said. "I'll check into those studies right away!"

"I'll be praying for you to find a new church and until then, I think you'll enjoy the studies I've suggested. Thanks so much for sharing your knowledge on the Civil War. I hope to come back when I have more time to explore." We said our goodbyes. And the urgency to give someone a message was gone.

This woman was definitely *the one*. As I settled in behind the steering wheel of my car, I could see that the Huntingdon's were still enjoying barbeque and watermelon. And I thanked the Lord I didn't feel the slightest urge to go over there and "exhort."

But back on the road headed for I-65 and the crab boil, I had another "word" with God. "Lord, why didn't you have someone from the Huntingdon family reunion go speak with this woman? Or someone from one of the many churches around here? Or that man with his son? I could have been waylaid by bandits and cutthroats this far out. Why would you have me leave the interstate and drive all this way…why *me?*"

Immediately I heard in my spirit, "Because of your passion for Civil War history and your passion for *me.*"

Oh, *now* the Lord was talking. Wow. Just wow.

And then I asked, "Then why couldn't you give me a hint about what I was supposed to be doing. Some clues! *Something*. I felt hung out to dry! I need strategic sandboxes if I'm going to be desert fighting. Battle plans. I need to know where to place my bazookas. You know you almost gave me a heart attack when I saw that family reunion going on. I could have had more help there—don't you think?"

And although I didn't want to hear it, what I heard next in my spirit made sense. "Faith." Evidently I didn't have enough. And He planned on building mine through trials.

Several other words began to flood into my spirit. *Obedience. Trust. Testing.*

"Okay, I get it. Guess I got a D+ on that test. But thanks for giving me the right words at the last minute anyway. I know you've allowed others to have even more difficult moments than I had back there. At least I didn't have the Red Sea in front of me and the Egyptian army breathing down my back. I really would have had a heart attack. You know deep water scares me. But one more thing, can I at least have a storm at sea while I'm in Destin? You know—one of those brilliant electrical storms that never comes inland to do damage but is such a spectacular show?"

Nothing. No more words of wisdom. Simply nothing. Why were all of my conversations with Him mostly one-sided? Sigh.

I turned the Christian radio station back on and kept my hood ornament pointed south.

The crab boil was just getting started when I arrived in Destin. I hadn't missed a thing. The beach and bicycling could wait until tomorrow.

Over buttered corn on the cob, sea fare, and crab-pot boiled potatoes, I was asked if I'd encountered a lot of traffic on the way down." I hesitantly replied, "Well, you wouldn't believe what happened right before Montgomery...."

"Traffic jam?"

Then I thought better of sharing something so personal and beautifully scripted by God. No one would believe what happened to me; only those who had totally free-fallen in abandonment for Christ and had experienced strange and questionable things too. I was like Mary in a sense, a girl who *kept all these things, and pondered them in her heart.* Luke 2:19 I simply wanted to bask in His presence. I even feared "what man would say." So I veered toward safety until I could later process the experience more fully. Alone.

I was in a jam alright. Let's just say it was bumper-to-bumper hair raising with a major bullet-dodging-detour.

I smiled. "It wasn't all *that* bad." And it struck me that no backside of a boondock is ever God-forsaken.

On my last night in Destin—God seems to enjoy last minute surprises—I got the answer to my Montgomery I-65 request. The desire of my heart. An electrical lightning storm at sea. Everyone else had gone to bed. All were asleep. My room happened to be on the second floor and as my head rested on my pillow in a bed situated in front of glass doors—drapes open—that opened up onto a balcony, I thought I was watching a private fireworks show. Simply majestic. If I'd been in one of the other guest rooms, I would have missed the display because the other guest rooms didn't have an ocean view. I couldn't have asked for more. All was silent except for my whisper:

"Thank you for giving me the desires of my heart, Lord."

On the way back to Tennessee with my daughter, the closer we came to Montgomery, the closer I came to sharing what had happened on my trip down. This child had once told her friends that her mom could communicate with birds—really embarrassing when I got asked about it...but there *was* that one bluebird on top of the wrought iron fence that actually flew back to hear more about what I was saying to him, cocking his head from side to side. Then, there *were* those migrant canvas back ducks down at the pond that seemed to understand my duck calls and quacked back when the mallards snubbed me.

But the Confederate Museum visit, and that attendant, and the word *church*... would my teen think her mom was a total nutcase? I took a chance and told her anyway. Then asked her if she believed the incident was a God-thing.

"I've been with you before when strange things happened," she said, adjusting her pillow. "This is nothing new. Strange things happen to you *all* the time, Mom. You talk to *birds*. And they talk *back*. Of course I believe it was a God-thing."

My brethren, count it all joy when ye fall into divers temptations; Knowing this, that the trying of your faith worketh patience." James 1:1-3

*The name on the family reunion banner has been changed.

11

Questionable Vacations

The trip started out like most vacations, but this time with three grandees age five years, three years, and five-months. I made sure to pack necessities for a picnic: sandwiches, drinks, fruit, Cheetos, paper towels, a table cloth, and Benadryl—Hayden, the eldest, already sounded like she had a cold.

Are we there yet was asked before we got out of town. Even though I'd let the girls choose pristine journals with pens before leaving my house, they were still restless. Moans could be heard from the back seat every time my daughter, Peyton, said, "We have six more hours to go. Watch your show or write in the journals Lovie gave you." Even though everyone had eaten breakfast, *I'm hungry* was said 100 times before lunchtime. And I reminded everyone that my parents used to take me to the beach in a car with no air conditioning and no pop-down screens for movies.

"I counted cars and cows for entertainment after we traveled in cars that had air conditioning."

I added, "When we see palm trees and smell the sea you'll know we're getting close."

When lunchtime rolled around, I gathered up the cooler and the white sheet I was using for a tablecloth for concrete benches at rest stops.

"Why do we have to have a tablecloth?" Hayden asked. A five-year-old who always piped up, her questions were endless.

"Because I refuse to eat on a dirty table, that's why," I responded while separating the PB&J from the PB only. "And when you get older," I said to three-year-old Harper, maybe you'll learn to love jelly on your PB sandwich and then lettuce and tomato on a BLT might sound delicious."

"Yuck!" Harper replied while baby Hope Ruby blew bubbles to pass the time as she rested in her mother's arms.

After a visit to the restrooms with me first admonishing the children to hold hands and never stray from my sight, all hands were washed and we hit the road again. From Tennessee, we were bound for the Emerald Coast along the Gulf of Mexico. And of course, after lunch and a Capri Sun, someone would have to potty again for a second time. No worries. Peyton had packed a portable potty.

A couple of hours later, Mother Nature called from the backseat. Harper said, "I need to go potty!" The only problem was finding a quiet, secluded place on the side of the road. Like magic, a First Baptist Church in Liberty, Alabama appeared on our right. Perfect. Because it wasn't a Sunday, the parking lot was empty. I pulled to the end of the parking lot near the woods for privacy and announced, "Okay. Harper's going to potty on Holy Ground. And in Liberty, Alabama." And I thought, *She will be liberated and free at last.*

Peyton said, "Mom, you didn't have to drive us into the bushes!"

"I'm only providing privacy," I replied, while wondering if God was going to tell us—like Moses—to take our shoes off.

When all was said and done, Peyton held up the plastic bag and asked, "What am I supposed to do with this? There are no trash cans."

"Well, you can't trash up holy ground," I replied. "Just empty the potty bag and we'll have to find another bag in the car to use as a trash bag for the potty bag." As I pulled the car onto the highway, Peyton pulled hand sanitizer from the console and I waved at the church and said, "Thank you and goodbye First Baptist—we watered your bushes for you!"

The Grandees giggled and giggled.

Once on the coast, the weather was perfect. Hurricanes had all cleared out. We couldn't wait to get our bathing suits on and put our feet in the sand and surf. And, we were excited about the children's dad, Chris, flying in to Panama City where he would make arrangements to Uber to Blue Mountain Beach to find us staked out under an umbrella near the surf.

These were halcyon days. Hayden and Harper "wrote" daily in their journals about their trip—Hayden recording Harper's use of the potty on Holy ground. There was plenty of Breyers Neopolitan ice cream and Popsicles, lots of delicious fried crab claws and crab cakes, a donut shop right around the corner, and beach shovels and buckets for building drip sand castles. Harper was only in time-out once for hitting Hayden with a shovel and later telling a woman at a restaurant in Seaside, "I pitched a big fit today!" The woman had replied, "You go girl. I was a middle child too, so you *own* those big fits."

If I didn't count my fright at seeing something that looked like a sea snake headed straight toward me in the clear Gulf water (turned out to be a skinny fish with a long snout that dodged me while I held in a shriek) all was lovely. Lovely, that is, until all of us came down with Hayden's cold on our last beach day. Even then, I stayed indoors for some peace and quiet and read a good book while every now and then raising my gaze to watch the ocean undulate back and forth with an ancient, mesmerizing rhythm and swell that always soothed my soul. Then came time for Hayden to fly back home with her Dad so she wouldn't miss school the next day and time for Peyton, Harper, baby Hope Ruby, and me to retrace our tire tracks back to Tennessee.

And of course, one last rest area picnic stop.

As Peyton and I sat at the picnic table eating our sandwiches while Hope Ruby patted her hands together and grinned, Peyton said, "Do you have an eyeball on Harper?"

I was confident Harper was perfectly fine because I'd already scanned the vicinity for snakes—something Daddy had taught me to always look for—before whipping out our table cloth. "She's right behind you sitting on a tree stump."

Harper seemed safe and content sipping her fruit punch approximately 25 feet away from us. The surroundings were serene, the blue sky was something to behold, and we were in no imminent danger. There were no strangers near, nothing to worry about, and my alert radar was muted. Until I heard Harper cry out.

Oh dear God! Could a snake have a den beneath the tree stump? I hate snakes!

When I looked up, the child's face registered sheer terror. She let out a murderous scream and ran to our picnic table as I threw my sandwich down and ran to meet her.

"What, Harper!" I yelled. "What is it?"

I couldn't comprehend what had happened until my gaze lowered and I took in her pink dress. A huge dark splotch didn't fit in with the fabric's color. Then the dark splotch moved and the realization hit me—ants. The child was covered with a mass of swarming fire ants. I grabbed her dress and tried jerking it off of her but she was bent over trying to fight the insects biting her ankles and legs and keeping me from getting the dress pulled free. *Oh God! Oh God!* I silently cried. And while this was happening, I worried about pulling the dress over her head in case the ants transferred to her face and hair.

Peyton yelled, "Take the baby!"

I snatched Hope Ruby from her mother and Peyton grabbed the skirt of Harper's dress and bellowed out a command worthy of a Swat team member, "Arms up!" With that order and Harper's obedience, only then was Peyton able to get the dress off of the horrified child and knock the ants off of her. Handing the baby off again to her mother, I knocked ants off of the pink dress, stomping and killing as many as I could find, while feeling like ants were crawling over every inch of my body.

"Benadryl!" Peyton yelled. "Run get the Benadryl!"

Running to the car, I quickly located the Benadryl, and for some odd reason, I thought of the hand sanitizer in the console and grabbed it too.

While Peyton juggled the baby and poured out a dosage of Benadryl, I slathered hand sanitizer all over the 30 fire ant bites that covered mostly Harper's ankles with a couple on her legs, and one on her arm.

"Why are you putting hand sanitizer on her bites?" Peyton asked, an incredulous look on her face.

Dumbfounded, I replied, "I don't know. The alcohol. Maybe the alcohol will keep the bites from becoming infected." I, too, was surprised by my actions and had no other reason for slathering on hand sanitizer, except for the fact that when I ran to the car, something—perhaps the Holy Spirit—was telling me to grab the hand sanitizer too.

I thought back to a phone call with Peyton the day before the trip. She'd said, "Mom, I'm headed your way. Please go to the grocery store and buy baby food and diapers. I didn't have time to go to the store before leaving town." Peyton hadn't said a word about Benadryl—she usually brought a medicine bag on trips that included everything the children might need. But while at the store, I'd been prompted to buy the antihistamine, somehow knowing I needed to take it, yet without knowing if any of the kids were sick. Of course God knew what was going to happen on this trip before it happened since He's omniscient. Had He been preparing me through His Holy Spirit?

Since He knew where the fire ants were and we'd be stopping there—and there was no hospital around in case Harper had a reaction to the bites—why hadn't He prevented Harper from sitting down in a fire ant nest? Where was her guardian angel? Questions. I had questions for God. *God, this is a child? Why did you let this happen to a child?*

I heard in my spirit, *Would you rather have suffered her pain instead?*

I thought, *Don't make me do this! No I don't want 30 fire*

ant bites all over me! I have three bites now and right on top of my little finger where I had my poison ivy outbreak this summer and you know it took me three weeks for the swelling to go down and for the patches to heal and the place is still sensitive! I don't need more pain!

But would you take the suffering instead of your grandchild?

Oh, the guilt! *Of course if it came down to it, you know I'd die for my loved ones. I can't believe we're discussing this right now. At. This. Time. I hardly ever hear from You directly and now you're asking me this? Yes, I would suffer all of Harper's fire ant bites, though truthfully, I really don't want to, God! Send an angel next time!*

And suddenly, Jesus waves came crashing in, reminding me of the pain He suffered for me. Here my skin was crawling just thinking about those devilish fire ant bites while Jesus was willing to take a nail—and took more than one—to save wretches like me. Made me loathe myself just thinking about my hesitation.

Why that back and forth with God at that particular time, I don't know. I'm not fond of those "come to Jesus" moments. Those moments when God totally circumcises the heart. Painful moments when questions come about the ultimate sacrifice.

I was worn out and ready to head back to Tennessee.

Later at home, I checked out Harper's ant bites. All were angry-red and swollen. I Googled a video on fire ants and found that big pustules would soon develop and it would take about seven days for them to get better. I also discovered that golfers carried hand sanitizer with them and doused fire ant bites with the solution so they wouldn't swell as badly and the golfers could play longer. The guy in the video said that even Windex was good to use since anything that had ammonia in it would help keep the swelling down, therefore, easing the pain. But if there was no ammonia handy, hand sanitizer would help. I then showed the video to Hayden and Harper so they would know what a fire ant nest might look like. Though most of the time a nest can hardly be seen, at least this incident would make them check out their surroundings before sitting down in the future.

After seeing the video and giving the recent happenings more thought, I was amazed. God hadn't prevented the traumatic event, but His Holy Spirit had whispered to me to buy Benadryl and then later had put the thought into my mind to grab the hand sanitizer to use to prevent Harper's condition from worsening.

And I thanked God, Harper had the Mother Nature potty break call on the way to Florida via Liberty, Alabama, and we'd quickly found the First Baptist Church parking lot on a lonely two-lane highway in the middle of nowhere. If it hadn't been for the potty break, I wouldn't have seen where Peyton kept her hand sanitizer.

I've said it before and I'll say it again, the Lord works in mysterious ways to teach His children lessons. Through His word there is *true* liberty. And I thank God almighty that through that liberty I am free at last!

But that's not the ending to this story. Harper never once scratched her fire ant bites, nor did they get infected. But within a day or so, all three children tested positive for strep throat! *Really Lord? No break for the weary?*

After texting a friend about all of the recent trials and tribulations, she sent me the day's radio broadcast from Dr. David Jeremiah. The main takeaway: Persevere. For perseverance builds character.

Lord, aren't we there yet?

~ 12 ~
Laying My Watery Ghosts to Rest

My mother talked about the *Titanic* every now and then. How horrific it was. The sad stories. The sacrifices. And when I was in high school, I read an article about the disaster, and wondered how anyone could think a ship was invincible. That was like tempting God and saying, "*I dare you to take me down.*"

When Mother passed, I found some of her newspaper clippings: articles about the Kennedy assassination, Elvis' marriage, and Grace Kelly, Princess of Monaco. I smiled when I saw the image of Grace Kelly. Mother always said my firstborn—a blonde—favored her.

But then, beneath Grace Kelly clippings, I saw it. An article about the *Titanic* sinking in 1912—several years before Mother was born. The article had been written many years after the sinking, but it still gave me goose bumps. Why was I so fascinated by this ship's sinking? I thought back on the first time I sailed on a cruise. I was journey proud. So excited to be vacationing on an actual ship with sails! A Windjammer Cruise leaving from the island of St. Maarten. I had new snorkeling equipment that I wanted to try out—my first time to snorkel. I had big plans to get over my fear of deep water. It was a fear I was anxious to overcome.

Plodding down the metal steps wearing mask and fins, I finally made it to the platform. The heavy swells of the ocean weren't what I'd expected. As the ship rose with each swell, so did the platform…like a New York skyscraper in the sky. Or so my vivid imagination thought. Those already in the water encouraged, "When the platform comes down closer to the water, jump!" Easy for them to say. If I jumped, how on earth would I ever get back on the platform? But I was determined to learn to snorkel so I stuffed my anxieties.

Once in the salty water, I found it easy to float. After arranging my mask, I put my head down and tried to see something. Nothing but darkness. Then I inhaled water and choked. Raising my head for air, I thought, *this is more complicated than I thought it would be.* Treading water, I looked around. The ocean swells seemed gigantic. I checked out the ship that could accommodate 120 people. As it tilted to the side with each wave, I could see more of the ship's bottom. And the water that seemed to be sucked up beneath the ship. The platform crashing back down into the sea unnerved me.

Panic inside me began to swell like a helium balloon. And with all of the commotion and water that seemed to only get rougher, I knew I had to get out of the inky dark sea and back on the platform. But how? If I tried to get back on the platform and it crashed down and hit me on the head, I might get a concussion and then sink to the bottom of the ocean. Oh, God. No! Just like the people who died when the *Titanic* sank.

Then I began thinking, the ship is going to suck me beneath

the hull. My fear was so great, every cell was saturated with panic. I swam over to the nearest guy and cat-clawed my way to the top of his head. "I have to get out!"

Not happy about this person who was trying to drown him, the other swimmer helped me over to the platform. Trying to grab the moving platform was like trying to jump into a Nike speed double jump rope game. I had my hands up and was waiting for the right time, however, I just couldn't get the rhythm down to "go."

Finally, the guy helping me—a man totally out of patience and same guy I'd tried to drown—told me I needed to go back to my room and practice in my bathroom's "head" before venturing into deep water again. Then with one hard shove from him that catapulted me into the air, I grabbed the platform and scrambled to safety. Never a good swimmer, I decided it might be best if I learned to snorkel in shallow water first. No way was I going to practice with my head in the toilet.

During that entire cruise and the few on much larger passenger ships I went on later, I would think about the *Titanic* and every other sea disaster I knew about. I made sure to learn how to buckle my life vest. Made sure to closely follow the drills as, before pulling up anchor, I and other passengers practiced for a possible mishap at sea. And when out at sea and the ride became bumpy and rough and tumble, I couldn't stop thinking about the *Titanic* and worrying.

But why was the *Titanic* so ingrained in my psyche? I finally reasoned it was because I knew so much about it from articles. And it was so sad. Wives saying goodbye to husbands. A wife staying with her husband to go down with the ship. I kept asking myself, *would I go down with the ship to stay with a loved one?* Drowning was my worst fear. My entire life, when I thought about something, anything, a story that someone else told me, a story I read, I visualized every scene, just like the *You Are There* movies shown to kids in elementary school. Without seeing the first *Titanic* movie, I'd already visualized the countenances of the people left on the ship to drown: Downcast eyes. Crying eyes. Sad eyes. Forlorn eyes. Desperate eyes. I could see those that smoked their last cigarette as they calmly prepared for death as best they could while the band played.

I could see the people trapped on the lower decks, running to higher ground trying to find a way of escape. And those poor men in the boiler rooms left to try and keep the ship running—how horrible to see them in my mind's eye rising to the top of the ceiling of their compartment as the water rose—taking their last breath against the paint of their coffin's roof.

For the people who tried to jump ship, I felt the horror of trying to get far enough away from the ship so the suction created by it sliding to the bottom of the ocean wouldn't drag them down in its wake. I could visualize them trying to fight the suction's vortex, clawing their way back to the surface. Some making it, some to be pulled deeper to watery graves.

And then those left in the boats that floated on still water—I felt their pain. Their loss. The stinging North Atlantic air as they shivered in what clothes they'd escaped in, listening to the pitiful cries of those who couldn't find a boat that wasn't overcrowded. I felt it all and the thought-scenes were stuck in cellular memory.

When virtual tours came out—simulators of the *Titanic*—I watched as if I was placing myself on that fateful ship and "learning the ropes" so to speak. Learning which corridors to take, where my cabin might have been, I always ended up at the helm, trying to warn the captain of the hour about the danger. To no avail. I couldn't change a thing. There was no rolling back time to prevent the tragedy.

Not until a few years ago was I able to read *A Night to Remember* by Walter Lord. A grown woman with grandchildren now, I finally forced myself to read that book when it jumped out at me in a second hand bookstore. Fifty cents. Not even a dollar for the lives lost. I felt ashamed I couldn't help shoulder some of the pain felt by the passengers who must have suffered from survivor's guilt. So I forced myself—literally forced myself—to read the book hoping to overcome my fear of the *Titanic* story, just as I had overcome my fear of deep water by learning how to snorkel and scuba dive. And in that book, I relived Lord's minute-by-minute account of the *Titanic's* final hours. He made those ghosts more alive to me than they already were. His recounting put flesh to those watery bones.

Even though reading that book was a major feat, I knew the ghosts still haunted me.

Recently, I was in Pigeon Forge at a retreat. Every day on my way to lunch I passed the Titanic Museum Attraction. Every day, I almost turned the wheel of my car to go in. But for some reason, I always shied away.

That time will surely come. The *Titanic* still calls me. I plan to conquer that *Titanic* fear just as I did my fear of deep water. Hopefully, I'll be able to visit the museum when Yvonne

Lehman is there signing her novel *Hearts That Survive*. Hopefully, with that visit, I'll finally be able to lay my watery ghosts to rest.

An addendum: This story was first published in 2017 in *Why? Titanic Moments*. As you will see with the next story, I was later able to be with Yvonne when she was at the museum during a book signing. I also toured the museum and, via *Titanic* Conferences, got to know several of the survivors' descendants who shared their ancestors' stories. What a privilege to be with all of these precious people!

Unfortunately, Yvonne left us to return to her heavenly home in 2021 to be with her Lord and Savior. Her positive energy and contribution to the Christian writing world is missed.

As for laying my watery ghosts to rest, discoveries are still being made regarding the *Titanic*. I'm not sure if we will ever know the truth behind the sinking of that majestic ship.

❧ 13 ❧
Together in the Daybreak

After writing my story for Yvonne Lehman's compilation *Why? Titanic Moments*, I thought I'd laid my watery ghosts to rest. That was before I received an invitation to the book signing for her novel *Hearts that Survive,* along with an invitation to a *Titanic* event at the Pigeon Forge *Titanic* Museum where Helen Benzinger, a descendant of the famous *Titanic* survivor Molly Brown, would be speaking along with Lyle Lowell who would be in character as Captain Smith. How could I pass up hors d'oeuvres and a 1912 dress up dinner party? At last I'd be turning my steering wheel to direct my car into the parking lot of the *Titanic* Museum Attraction. Something I hadn't been able to do, as noted in my last epistle.

But there I was at last. And a marvelous time was to be had by all who attended the magnificent event. I managed to overcome my fears of *Titanic* memories from childhood that had lingered into adulthood. And I discovered to my delight that the museum was a marvel to behold and very tastefully designed with displayed artifacts and recreated rooms.

So, for a lack of better words, I thoroughly enjoyed the event, helped Yvonne for a New York Minute with her book signing, and thought I was done.

Then came an invitation to another *Titanic* event, one that would include more talks from descendants whose ancestors had survived the sorrowful night in April 1912. Was I turning into a Titaniac? No one had tempted with hors d'oeuvres, yet after Yvonne emailed that the event might be something I would find interesting I found myself signing up for Bill Willard's 2017 conference in Pigeon Forge. What more could I learn about that fateful night I didn't already know or care about?

As it turned out, there were tons of facts and stories I'd not yet heard about. My research and reading had barely touched the tip of the iceberg—and please pardon that horrid pun. For instance, Bill Sauder, researcher for the *RMS Titanic* project, raised a couple of questions about how the ship sank. From photos and videos taken at the wreckage site, it became known that, indeed, the boat broke apart somewhere near midship. But did the bow nosedive all of the way to the bottom in a death spiral or did it invert at some point? Or perhaps it had floated down with a more gentle stair-step bumping until it reached its final resting place? Sauder said it was necessary to give the scatter field the "Sherlock Holmes Treatment." There were clues. Because there was still an upright dish on a cabinet and definite markings from the disturbance of the mud and sediment, it could easily be deduced that the bow floated down in a more gentle stair-step bumping motion.

And how did the stern sink? And in what relationship to the bow? So many clues if one knew what to look for. Interestingly enough, it made perfect sense the site of the sinking would be defined by where the five boilers rested since they were heavy and would have taken the fastest path to the ocean floor, their location agreeing with the longitude and latitude of the ship's exact sinking.

All of these tidbits were extremely interesting, but I decided that instead of being so much a "Lifeboat Person" or "Rivet Counter," I was more a "Passenger People." The people of the *Titanic* called me from the deep. What did they see? What did they feel? What were their last words? Why were there discrepancies in some stories? And mainly, what were their personal stories about their families and lives before and after *Titanic*?

Testimonies were recorded on the *Carpathia* after the survivors were safely aboard and tended to, and the rescuing ship started for New York with her "load of sorrow and woe and misery." Yet stories seemed to change going into the American and British inquiries. For instance, one survivor said she saw the shooting of a steerage passenger, yet later she either retracted her statement or failed to go on record to stand by her original recorded observation. Would the ship's officers have been found guilty of murder if indeed they'd killed passengers? Could that be why her story had changed?

Admittedly, some of the ship's officers had guns. Gunshots were heard. Other witnesses said a couple of men from steerage who rushed the lifeboats were shot by Officer Murdoch. And did Murdoch commit suicide after shooting these men? Or, as some thought, was it Captain Smith who reportedly committed suicide? The only way of knowing about suicides were if the bodies had been found and gunshot wounds were detected.

I read in one account that some of the passengers on the

ship also had guns and committed suicide rather than drown or freeze in the frigid sea. What happened to those who might have committed suicide at "dark bloody thirty in the morning" is still a mystery because many of the bodies were never found.

Some accounts though, are not a mystery. Some words can never be forgotten. Frank Goldsmith Jr.—descendant of Frank Goldsmith Sr. who was nine years old at the time of the sinking—shared some private moments from that fateful night. "My Dad was so excited he was going to the land of Cowboys and Indians. My grandmother had taken her Singer sewing machine wrapped up in a folded carpet. They left Southampton, England to board a ship that was the length of three football fields, and they were inspected for head lice and pink eye before being allowed to take their place in the Third Class section of the ship. My father, Frankie, played posse with other kids all over the ship until they were run out of one area into the next. At one point in their play, they were close enough to the workers below that they heard rhythmic chanting as the men shoveled coal to keep the ship running."

Though Frank brought his grandparents' story back to life in such a vivid way, I was completely unprepared to hear his voice crack and see him choke up when he told of the separation of his father's family. As his grandfather was about to be torn from his wife and son so "women and children only" could be boarded into the lifeboats, this father's farewell to his son was: "So long Frankie, I'll see you later." As Frank teared up telling of a grandfather he never had a chance to meet due to fate, he finally managed to get out, "It still gets to me even now."

When Frank composed himself, he was able to share that his father said that as the lifeboat descended to the glassy sea, he could see inside a port hole where stewards and maids were playing around and smoking, and he was thinking, "They're going to get into trouble because they're not supposed to be smoking."

Later, a safe distance from any suction the ship might cause on its death plunge, Frank's grandmother grabbed his father and covered his eyes as the band onboard played the song "Autumn." Frankie managed to pull away to see the ship as it sank into the depths of the sea.

For the adult "Frankie," now known by the more staid name of "Frank," springtime was a challenge and a time when relatives and friends gave him a wide, but loving, berth. He avoided ballgames because to him the crowds' cheering sounded like the roars and sounds made by those who were dumped into the ice-cold waters without life jackets or lifeboats, and therefore had no chance for survival.

Other stories were told at the 2017 conference by descendants of survivors. Julie Hedgepeth Williams had an Uncle Al who survived the disaster. Shelley Binder had an ancestor by the name of Leah who suffered for 11 months in and out of mental institutions after the tragedy. She'd had her baby torn from her arms and they weren't immediately reunited. As if it wasn't enough that she struggled mentally, emotionally, and physically while aboard a row boat before their reunion, she had to reconcile herself to the fact that she'd lost her child, yet she herself had been saved. Later, aboard the *Carpathia*, her story played out like another horror tale of

Biblical proportions. With the *Carpathia's* doctor playing King Solomon, Leah had to prove a little boy in another woman's arms was truly her son. Because Leah's family was Jewish, the child could be identified by his circumcision along with an identifying birthmark no one else would have known about. With this information, the doctor deemed the baby should be returned to his rightful mother immediately.

If those stories weren't enough to ponder, the conference was chockfull of other speakers with their own stories. There was never a boring minute. Yet the finale was one I wasn't prepared for and I was caught off guard. When Bill passed out lyrics to a couple of songs written by Robin Gibb (Bee Gees) and his son R. J. Gibb and played their CD for a "Titanic Requiem—In Remembrance," I read the first line of the song "Daybreak": "My soul surrenders to the lonely sea...."

Glancing up at my tablemates I said, "Oh. No. I'm in trouble." I met Yvonne's gaze and said, "We're going to need tissues." Mild understatement. I would need an entire box but managed to dig around in my purse to find only one slightly used sheet.

When Bill's voice broke a couple of times as he projected on the wall different family photos of those who'd had the misfortune to purchase tickets for passage on the *Titanic*, he finally managed to croak out, "These people have become like family." He added, "Their lives changed in just a matter of hours."

I tried to choke down sobs while thinking, "I did not sign up for this part!" and thought I might have to bolt from the room through the door next to me as I saw those somber parents with cherubic faced babies and toddlers—real, precious souls I knew hadn't made it through their darkest night of the soul. By the time the "remembrance" was over, my tissue was soaked and in knotted shreds. And I was still weeping while daubing at mascara with my fingers to keep black streaks from running down my chin.

Bill was correct in his summation. Those who were lost on the *RMS Titanic* had become like family. So had the other conference attendees. I'd never participated in a conference where I felt so bonded before time to return home. But this group of passionate and knowledgeable people had met me on the first day at the "Meet and Greet" like I was no stranger and one of them. And no matter if it was dark-bloody-thirty-in-the-morning somewhere and I had another copious weeping jag, I knew they could sympathize because I couldn't help but hear some of their more covert sniffles. It was understood they were touched as much as I.

By the time we parted, I knew I would be seeing them again somewhere along the *Titanic* sea lanes. There were too many more mysteries to solve and so many more stories to uncover. And we hoped to do it "together in the daybreak."

~ 14 ~
When Joy Finally Comes

"The tumor on his lung is the size of my fist," Daddy's internist said, holding his fist up to the X-ray. "See that dark spot there. He has four months to live."

I heard the Holy Spirit's soft whisper, "Three months."

Thanking the doctor, I turned to leave. The bad news would be delivered later to the patient.

I almost worried myself to death during the next hours. I knew Daddy wouldn't want to go to a nursing home. He'd always planned to stay in his home until the bitter end. And he'd always been terrified of hospitals. The smell of hospitals terrified him as well. I knew the upcoming months would be long and hard.

The time to tell him finally arrived.

"Who says I'm dying?" Daddy demanded.

Confused, I replied, "Your doctor. He showed me the X-ray. You have a tumor the size of your fist on one lung. Daddy, I just want you to know, I'll try my best to take good care of you." Speaking while wiping away spilling tears, I added, "When the cancer progresses, Hospice will come to the house when needed. You won't be alone. You'll be taken care of."

The next days were difficult. Daddy vacillated back and forth about his imminent death. One minute he couldn't believe he was dying. The next minute he was down in his coffee dregs. We'd already planned his funeral years earlier. I'd even helped him choose the songs that would be sung during the service. And I promised he'd have the same funeral he'd given Mother—down to the vault she was buried in. One that was guaranteed not to leak. He was as prepared as anyone could be, considering death wasn't a lovely thing to think about and one could never be totally reconciled with leaving this world when one was leaving precious family behind.

When he finally came to grips with the fact that cancer was getting the best of him, there was one thing he couldn't shake: the pain in his back that wouldn't go away. And he eventually asked for the prescribed pain pills.

The days consisted of watching movies. Nonstop war movies. "A Bridge Too Far" was one of his favorites. He'd been in the first wave of boats to cross the river with machine gun fire mowing down everyone in his boat but himself and one other. I helped him fight WWII all over again. "Heaven Knows, Mister Alison" starring Robert Mitchum was a war movie that I loved as well. When I wasn't singing along with Robert Mitchum, "Don't sit under the apple tree with anyone else but me," I cooked Dad's favorite meals.

He requested salmon patties cooked the way Mother used to prepare them. Fried okra and squash were other favorite foods. One day, he asked for cornbread crumbled into a glass of milk—a treat he'd always loved. Every day he wanted ice cream. He got it. Boat loads. And every day he wanted his pain pills. I doled his meds out too. Until the hospice nurse said he'd better go slow on the pain medication because the pain might get much worse during his final days and they wouldn't work their magic if his body craved more than the pills could deliver. So, Daddy went cold turkey on the pain pills all together.

Then one day, I heard the old soldier say, "I'm tired of fighting that war. I don't want to watch any more war movies. Can you fix me a soft egg?"

So, with soft eggs scrambled, we watched "Gone with the Wind." Over. And over. The movie was Mother's favorite. Perhaps he was preparing himself see her again, real soon.

The pastor came to visit one day and asked me for a few private moments alone with him. I knew he was going to ask Daddy if he was ready. If he'd made his peace with his Lord. I'd already asked. And Daddy said, "Yes. I'm sure of my salvation. I believe Jesus died for my sins." But I let the pastor have his time anyway while I walked the road to the barn. Standing there next to the hot wire, I looked out at the cattle watching me. And I began singing "Amazing Grace." They came, one by one. And stood before me all in a row. Like they knew what was happening back there in the house. Like they were grieving with me. Or at least showing respect. That's what I pretended to believe anyway. In reality however, they were only curious youngsters watching a human who lived in a foggy haze during those long torturous days and nights.

Finally, back in the house, and with the pastor out of earshot, Daddy said, "Why did you stay outside so long?" He was fearful of being left alone, especially with people he wasn't that familiar with. He'd always been shy.

How could I say, "I needed a break from the sadness."

"I'm here Daddy," I replied. "I'm here now."

The time came for a hospital bed to be brought in, along with a GEO-mattress to help prevent bedsores. Not long after, solid food was no longer needed. Ensure had taken its place as Daddy's only food source. Shortly after the last container of Ensure, Daddy went into a coma with only his breathing, now noticeable, letting me know he was still partly alive. I thought about Robert Mitchum dying of lung cancer. I thought of a couple of things that Mitchum and Daddy had in common: cigarette smoking and lung cancer.

That night, with Jasper, my Yorkshire Terrier, settled on the reclining chair next to me, I heard my fur baby yelp. Strange. I'd never heard him yelp like that before. He usually whined when he needed to go outside to relieve himself. I'd already taken him outside to take care of his business and couldn't believe he needed to potty again. Looking up at the sky, I noticed how dark the night was. Inky black. And I knew it wouldn't be long until Daddy was being escorted to heaven.

"Jasper," I said, "you're not even serious about doing anything. Hurry up so we can go back inside. It's freezing out here." Nothing. Jasper sniffed around, doing everything but what he was supposed to be doing. "That's it buddy. Rattlesnakes out here can swallow you whole. And they've been known to stick their heads out in winter. We're headed back to bed."

Back inside the great room, I settled in the recliner again with Jasper next to me. But something was amiss. I heard the sounds of the GEO mattress a foot from me but I no longer heard the labored breathing of my father. Suddenly, it dawned on me that Daddy had already passed through the veil. Jasper's previous yelp was one of fright as he must have witnessed or sensed the angels taking Daddy before him.

And just like that, Daddy had been whisked away in spirit three months after his cancer diagnosis, never to return to earth in the flesh. His earthly days of fighting were over. Faced with death and what was before me, I left my recliner and reached for Daddy's wrist to check his pulse. Then I checked his legs, just as Hospice had instructed. All of the splotchy purple signs of death were there. Indeed, he was gone. But what should have been a time for rejoicing was a time of sadness. Only after Hospice arrived, did the floodgates finally open. And then, only for a short time. Too much had to be done to spend time weeping.

Many weeks later, still missing my father, I stood beneath his apple trees and watched the cattle in the pasture. I couldn't help but softly sing, "Don't sit under the apple trees with anyone else but me...." I couldn't stop thinking about him. One night, he visited me in a dream. I asked, "Daddy, is heaven all you thought it would be? Are you happy now?" He replied, "Yes." Then he was gone.

When morning came and I remembered the dream, I also recalled the verse Psalm 30:5: *Weeping may tarry for the night, but joy comes with the morning.*

Now, more than ever, I know those words to be true.

Many years afterward, when I was writing this story on my laptop, I suddenly smelled the scent of tobacco. Daddy was a Winston cigarette smoker and had smoked from his youth. A memory from the past rushed into my mind: Daddy taking a fresh pack of cigarettes and with his right hand holding the pack, he tapped it against his left palm three times before tearing off the plastic casing. When the first cigarette was pulled out, the tobacco scent assailed my senses. I couldn't help but wonder—*Daddy are you with me?*

Several years ago while I was writing, I caught a whiff of White Shoulders perfume—a scent Mother often wore—and said aloud, "Mother, is that you? Are you here?" Nothing. When I get to heaven and I'm reunited with my parents, I hope I can remember to ask them if they ever visited me for a short while here on earth.

❧ 15 ☙
The Humbling Words

God has a way of reaching people and speaking to them through their interests—a good way to make a child of God sit up and take note.

Though I'd felt God's presence on several occasions in my life, I'd yet to hear His clarion call. A defining moment for me occurred when I was atop a horse in Scotland. During a jumping exercise, the students were instructed to ride their horses through a series of six in-and-out jumps, which meant the horse jumped one jump, bounced, then jumped, bounced, until all jumps were completed in that way. No problem. My horse was push button and well trained making me look like a fairly accomplished rider.

For the next exercise, we were told to drop the buckled reins on the horse's neck, hold our arms out to our sides, and jump the same jumps on balance using only our legs and dropped heels. The girl in front of me turned around with saucer-shaped eyes and said, "I'm not doing that! They're going to get us killed!"

I replied, "Well, please move your horse out of the way. I am. I paid good money to come over here and ride. If I die, ship my body back to the States with a note pinned to my corpse that says, 'She died with a smile on her face.'"

Completing the jumping exercise with perfection, I was filled with false pride as I cantered my horse around to fall back in line. Until I heard *The Humbling Voice* speak the *humbling words*. A clearly male voice that was not still and small but still gentle said, "You have jumped out of an airplane, rafted wild rivers, and now risked your life riding this horse over these jumps. Why won't you risk your life for me? I died for you."

The hair on my arms sprang to attention and my legs grew water-weak as I turned in the saddle to search behind me for the one who had spoken. Who was the joker claiming he'd died for me and how did he know my past? I was in a foreign country and no one knew me. Absolutely no one was near. And I could see no males on the ground level in the arena.

The girl who had refused to jump was ahead of me and when I approached she said, "Well, if you can do it, I can do it." I sat on my horse speechless—but not from her statement—as she and her horse took off. Who had spoken those words? Jesus Christ?

No. Way. Who. Would. Believe. This. ?

In the early 1900s and before, women were institutionalized for being too spiritual and reading their Bibles overly much. In fact, women were institutionalized if their husbands wanted to replace a wife with a younger woman or if their fathers had no sons and wanted a nephew to inherit instead of a daughter. Saying she heard the voice of Jesus Christ would definitely get a woman committed if a spouse needed an excuse.

Who in the world would believe Jesus was speaking to me? They'd think I'd lost my ever-loving mind. My next reaction was to feel like a heel, because Jesus *had* given his life for me. The guilt piled on.

"Oh, no. My fun is over. Could it be I'm getting called to the tropics to eat fried bologna and fend off gargantuan roaches while wearing really ugly missionary shoes? Been there and done that with the bologna and roaches." I'd seen the tire tread sandals…I was totally into black…but….

Maybe…if I *had* to….

Hearing nothing else, I struggled to make sense of what I had heard. I prayed, "Lord, is that you? If it is and you're calling me…*of course it's you*…can I go someplace where there's colder weather? You of all people know I hate to sweat. Oh no. *Russia*." I'd seen movies. I'd talked to a woman whose family had escaped from there by wagon. They'd hidden beneath the hay it carried while miraculously avoiding slashing bayonet checks.

Hmmmm. Mission work definitely had its excitement along with the drawbacks.

I kept thinking about that voice all day. Later, during a sidesaddle riding class, a devilish mare bit my hand, which did nothing to soothe my feelings. Where was my guardian angel protection?

I'll admit I got pretty sassy after that bite. "Oh, you're calling me but you're not protecting me?"

That evening, tired and so sore I could hardly walk, I held onto the stair railing with my one good hand and pulled myself up the back stairs of the Gleneagles hotel to my room for room service and a tub full of hot water.

What in the world did the owner of that voice want me to do? Hadn't I mentored prisoners at Brushy Mountain? Hadn't

I taught children's Bible classes? Hadn't I volunteered at the hospital with a real dead man's bones to teach kids about nutrition? Hadn't I given brown paper bags filled with food to the church pantry to give the unwashed every week? Hadn't I been a good daughter and helped my aging parents when they were sick? Hadn't I given money? Hadn't I bought and donated clothes to the poor? Hadn't I given Bibles to those who didn't have one? Hadn't I…what more did God want? *Hadn't I done enough for awhile? I was doing more than most! Couldn't I take a vacation and have some fun every now and then? Even the Apostle Paul took a couple of cruises!*

I heard no more voices. Not even still small ones. I didn't need to. The answer was evident. God wanted more than works. He wanted *all* of me. And He wanted me to totally trust him—my abject failure. When my babies were born, I couldn't dedicate them to the Lord for fear he would take them away. I didn't feel I was one who could bear up well if something debilitating happened to my children or worse, they were to be called back Home. I couldn't totally depend on God because I thought I could protect my children and do everything myself. And the thought of sending a child off to live with a prophet?

Not happening. My name was not Hannah.

I was holding out because I was trying to ease through life with no scraped knees. I was afraid that if I became a blip on God's radar screen He would shatter me. And I certainly knew that the devil doesn't come after those who sit warming pew benches. To step up for Christ was like wearing a T-shirt that reads, "Satan's Been Given Permission to Have a Go, Kick Me."

After I heard that clarion call from Jesus, He allowed me a time of Moses copouts. "Send Annette. I'm not worthy. I'm not equipped. You made a mistake. You're talking to the wrong wretched person." I imagined violins playing in heaven throughout my pity party.

Jesus was like His Father. Patient and kind. What I hadn't counted on was that the Lord is truly a man of His word. He equips through his Holy Spirit—Counselor and Comforter—before He opens doors.

After many times of throwing out the fleece like Gideon, I finally learned to listen for that still small voice and to trust Him. Did I sometimes still have wonky days when things went wrong? Of course. But I fell back on His other promises: "I will never leave you, nor will I forsake you."

The rest of the story… Not wanting to withhold anything from me, God graciously gave me the trials and tribulations He promised would come. I began writing. Literary works. God had other plans. He made it clear He wanted me writing for Him so I could share about those trials and tribulations and how I weathered them with courage while leaning on Him. Yes, my Father does have a sense of humor all His own—which I inherited. As for the kids, I jokingly and lovingly turned them back over to God when they hit their teens and informed Him, "You can have them back. They're all yours. This is where courage comes in handy. If you need a break, I'll be here 'til you call me home." I pictured Him on His throne—grinning big.

Oh, yeah, one more thing—I've acquired a taste for fried bologna but still abhor roaches and biting mares, tend to be too spiritual for some, still read my Bible overly much, and so far, have managed to keep from being institutionalized. Mwah-hah-ha-ha!

Wonders never cease.

~ 16 ~
Words of Validation

Every year during mornings in May, the Tufted Titmouse decked out in their gray tuxedos chirped, "Peter, Peter, Peter," while my flower garden was transformed. "Laughter" roses bloomed orange with yellow centers. "Old Blush" popped out along the white wooden fence inside my secret garden, inching her way to chat with pink and yellow "Marie Van Houte" and "Souvenir de la Malmaison" who was the biggest showoff of all.

Iris guarded the serenity of my land of enchantment with their sword-like leaves standing proud while pansies smiled with faces waiting to unveil wintry stories. Large, heavy, pink peonies bowed down in worship and clematis burst forth purple brilliance as the delicate but sturdy vine wound around the church birdhouse waiting for a new crop of Eastern blues.

It was on such a morning as this I first saw her—a lovely lady attending my Bible study class. Before leaving my garden, I'd cut Marie Antoinette's favorite climbing rose and now mine, "Souvenir de la Malmaison," and wrapped the stems of the pink roses in wet paper towels. Pinching aluminum foil around the stems, I formed a collar around each flower, then tied lavender colored ribbon around the middle of the stem below the foil collar to create a dainty bow.

On this special morning of gathering, I had given these small treasures away to friends and had one left over.

When the lady in front of the classroom spoke up to answer a question, I realized I'd never seen her before. She was so enthusiastic, so on fire for the Lord, and she glowed, as though the Holy Spirit beamed through her. I had to know this woman. After class, I introduced myself and presented her with my last gorgeous pink "Souvenir de la Malmaison" rose.

Smiling from ear lobe to ear lobe, Jordie finally said, "You remind me of a woman I know who has a rose ministry. She had been to a conference and was showered with a dozen long stem roses. On her journey home, she knew the roses would wilt before arriving so she made a decision to re-gift the flowers."

As the story unfolded, I learned that at one rest area on the interstate, the rose lady spotted a woman working at what normally was considered a man's job — mowing the rest area grounds with a tractor and large mower pulled behind. Hot beneath a scalding sun, the worker had taken a break to use the restroom and swallow a drink of water. Skin that had turned to a leathery brown from the sun's rays matched forlorn eyes that declared she was tired physically and emotionally.

As I listened to Jordie, it was here in the story this hardworking woman clearly popped into my mind. She was a possible descendant of a Scots-Irish immigrant and I could see her and her ancestors throughout their journeys.

Perhaps she was descended from a woman who had left Scotland for Northern Ireland in hope of better land and a better life after the clans were defeated by the English at the battle of Culloden in the 1700s. But because of religious persecution, potato crop failures, and a need to feed her family, she and her husband finally left Ireland on a ship headed for America and the Promised Land—Virginia soil that produced tobacco money.

Once relocated, she'd fled by horseback from an Indian massacre, escaping across a swollen river, mourning the dead left behind. What descendants remained finally made their way down the Great Wagon Road through North Carolina where the rich river land had already been taken—again by the English—people some of her kin would marry.

From the Yadkin River Valley, more descendants pioneered further south into Tennessee when the land was doled out by grants to Revolutionary War soldiers. And when the earth grew tired of growing corn and tobacco, some descendants ventured by flatboat from Tennessee to Alabama by way of the Tennessee River, and even deeper south or west by wagon.

But now, the young descendant farthest down the branch of her family tree was begging her husband to take her back north before malaria took every child she'd labored to birth, struggled to nurse, and prayed through Bright's disease, the bloody flux, pneumonia, malaria and worms that threatened every breath. She'd received word another relative had been massacred by Indians on her way to Fort Nashborough to buy cloth for a gown for her unborn child. The teeming frontier and its dangers frightened even the strong and the brave.

The lines etching this woman's thin face that harbored genes from many generations past spoke of loneliness, hardship, and heart sorrow of the deepest kind. She looked as though the only flowers she'd ever held were wild violets and daisies she'd picked as a barefoot toddler in mountain meadows not long before river bottom cotton bolls cut and scarred young tender hands.

Needing living water in the worst way to nurture her spirit, burdens that had become too heavy to bear had long ago sagged flour-sack draped shoulders that had stood seasons of menstrual floods and the drag of a 50-pound bag full of cotton headed for the gin and a wealthier woman's ample girth.

And now, this woman's daughter was a child who suffered from starvation during the War Between the States when all of the men had left their homes to fight on some of the bloodiest battlefields history ever recorded. With mules and horses confiscated by both armies, leaving fields unplowed for crops, the land lay as barren as this precious darling's dried up womb and hardened heart. How would she fight off the ravaging carpetbaggers without ammunition? She learned to sleep with an axe beneath her bed.

Yet, through all adversity, she made do when hogs were butchered by foraging soldiers so there was no meat for winter, the only green vegetable to be had was picked wild growing next to a creek or river, and coffee was ground from acorns if the squirrels didn't scavenge them first.

And to her, a granddaughter was born who would see many inventions and new developments, even the birth of a nation, Israel, on one 1948 May day—the day the Jewish people gained back their homeland, the land promised by God to Abraham's descendants.

This daughter never dreamed in a million years that the

man she married—the son of a long line of preachers—would turn to alcohol binges to ease his Great Depression pain. Or, that she would be forced to sit on a table and sing or else be beaten on the legs by the buckle of a belt if she tired of singing during her husband's latest whiskey-induced stupor. "Sing! Sing!"

And as she sat there and obeyed the head of the household as she had been taught she should, she sang "Precious Lord, take my hand, lead me on, let me stand, I am tired, I am weak, I am worn; Through the storm, through the night, lead me on to the light, take my hand, precious Lord, lead me home."

When the man she'd wed continued to threaten with the belt buckle if she tired, slowed, or needed to help her young, impressionable granddaughter eat her supper, she softly crooned, "I come to the garden alone while the dew is still on the roses, and the voice I hear falling on my ear, the Son of God discloses. And He walks with me, and he talks with me, and He tells me I am His own; And the joy we share as we tarry there, none other has ever known."

And I'm sure she thought that when she did at last tarry with Jesus, her Lord and Savior, even though she had finally divorced herself from her abusive husband, Jesus would touch the belt-buckle scars on her swollen ankles and heal them as she and her Christ shared limitless joy while her Savior whispered, "Beloved, you are my own. Walk with me in my garden of roses. You are the special bride I've always waited for. I will give you the roses you were never given and more than dew, I will give you My living water."

Brought back to the present, I heard Jordie ending the Rose Lady's story: "When a blood-red, long stemmed rose was handed to the rest area worker along with the words 'Jesus loves you,' her face beamed."

I envisioned her eyes transforming from a dull listlessness to shiny orbs of hope.

I was told, "As the rose lady prepared to pull out of the rest area, she noticed that the recipient of the rose had climbed back on the tractor and had begun to mow again. However, now, instead of a fallen countenance, her shoulders were thrown back, her head lifted and proud as her hand thrust the single rose in victory and 'thank you' to the blue sky and God in heaven above."

For now, the worker knew she wasn't forgotten—that God had sent a messenger to affirm she was worthy. She was someone of importance. She belonged. And the simple words, "Jesus loves you," were cherished in her heart and etched into the lines of her previously-lined brow. It was obvious to all, she knew without a doubt, she was a daughter of God Almighty, bride of Christ Jesus the King, God's Son.

The rose lady saw such an incredible transformation brought about from the red of a rose that she was reminded of the blood that drained with all of its life giving attributes from Jesus' body so the people of the world could all be saved if they so chose to accept Christ as Lord and Savior.

And from a single shared red rose accompanied by the spoken words, "Jesus loves you," the Rose Lady's rose ministry was launched.

The rest of the story: While researching ancestors of Scots-Irish relatives, I discovered some of the above stories in my genealogy. The wonderful grandmother with scarred ankles never spoke about her mistreatment by a man far gone in his cups, addicted to the poison that would soon destroy him. Her story wasn't found in a history book but was shared by an older cousin—the only tender-aged witness to a night's cruelties caused by a man who'd lived on the cusp of a life in a South still recovering from a lost war fought decades in the past, a South filled with failed crops and missed opportunities, a region of a country still struggling from the repercussions of decisions made by those who held men's fate and destinies in the palms of their hands. The same man who leaned on a bottle to help him cope instead of leaning on the everlasting arms of One who longed to embrace him and give him living water instead of water transformed into a liquid that would addle a brain into thinking he was on top of the world for a few short hours of foggy bliss.

That grandmother, along with another grandmother, were praying women who gave me my first Bibles and spoke these words, "Jesus loves you." I am extremely grateful for the strong godly women—lovers of peonies and roses—God placed in my life. And I keep the lyrics of the two special songs the one grandmother sang during her hours of suffering, "In the Garden" by C. Austin Miles and "Take My Hand, Precious Lord" by Thomas A. Dorsey, taped in the back of my Bible as a reminder of the sacrifices she made and the pain she'd once endured.

As for the woman who received a rose from the Rose Lady along with the words "Jesus loves you," she was validated by a stranger and made to feel like her life was worth something. Sometimes, powerful words of validation spoken from someone else wayfaring through this world are needed. Because indeed, those who are lost or those who are in pain trying to make it through one more day or one more tortuous and knotty night need to know they count. They matter. They are loved. They can endure and overcome. They need to hear the spoken words, "Jesus loves you," because those are words powerful enough to save. Those are words that are powerful enough to move mountains.

Hereby perceive we the love of God, because he laid down his life for us.... 1 John 3:16

~ 17 ~
A Battle with the Mouse King

Thinking back, I couldn't recall too many difficulties in teaching a two-year-old to stay in her own bed. But every single night I was in Hayden's (my first grandchild) home, tucked away in the grandmother room, Hayden crept to my door to turn the handle. Even after—in my bed—I read at least two books, flossed teeth, let her sing along to a YouTube video of Matt Redman singing "10,000 Reasons (Bless the Lord)" and then transferred her to her bed to sing a couple of other songs like "Jesus Loves Me" and "Do Your Ears Hang Low," talked about the favorite part of her day and the worst part of her day, gathered all of her stuffed animals into her bed's pillow corral, then said a prayer—ending with Je t'aime ("I love you" in French) and "Sleep tight. Don't let the bed bugs bite"—the child was determined to sneak back into my bed for the night. "I want to sleep in your bed, Lovie!"

Trying my best to obey parental rules, every time she opened my door, I sent her back to her own bed. Once, she opened the door so silently, I didn't hear her because I was working on my laptop. When I finally looked up to see her standing in the doorway with a determined look on her face, she said, "Lovie, you need to go to sleep!" Chastised by a two-year-old, I wondered why she thought I needed to go to sleep. I had work to do. *She* needed to go to sleep! What a challenge it was to get her down for the night.

Later, it would finally dawn on me that if I was asleep, I couldn't hear her sneak into the room to creep into my bed to have an all night snuggle bunny.

Quite the crafty one.

One night, after Hayden had come back into my room because she needed to put on her lips (ChapStick), then come again to potty, then come again to _____ (you fill in the blank with 10,000 reasons), she came to my room the last and final time. I decided to put my grandmother foot down.

However, the look on her face was so troubled, she looked so bereft, with such a waif-in-need-of-love crinkled up look on her bitty brow, that I couldn't bear it when she said, "Lovie, I'm sad." With that, my heart melted, and my arms opened wide as she rushed to my bedside with the ever present Honey Bunny I'd given her when she was born—the bunny she couldn't sleep without. The same bunny we searched the house for every night and naptime so she could drift off into bunny sleeping land so there would be no wailing or mourning in Beulah Land.

Putting down the book I was reading, I said, "Precious, why are you sad?" She'd now just turned three—could someone be bullying her in pre-school or did she have the entire world's weight on her shoulders—what could have this child so depressed? Had she seen something violent on T.V.?

While picking at her Honey Bunny, worrying the one

thread that hung down from Honey Bun's well-washed but now ragged looking satin trim, Hayden rushed out, "I want to be in 'The Nutcracker' like Mommie was when she was a little girl!"

Thank the Lord. Something I could fix. She'd seen the photos of her mother and me after a "Nutcracker" performance and she longed to be like Mommie.

"Honey, don't you worry," I assured her. "We can make that happen." She had just begun to take dance lessons and by the time she was old enough, she would be an easy shoe-in for local "Nutcracker" performances. Tiny dancers were always in demand.

"But Lovie," Hayden continued with eyes big as hoot owls', "I'm scared."

"Scared?" I said. "What are you afraid of—it's only a dance performance, Sweetheart. Like a play. Make believe."

Hayden pulled at Honey Bunny's string a couple more quick pulls before she could at last bare her troubled soul.

If possible, her eyes grew even bigger. "Lovie, I'm afraid of mice!"

I choked back my laughter, not wanting to make light of her fears. Even I was afraid of a rat.

It finally dawned on me that Hayden might have seen The Nutcracker performance on television during the Christmas holidays. And there was that ferociously fierce battle with "The Nutcracker" Prince and the Mouse King…when the toys came to life. Ahhhh. And there was that larger than life—to a little girl—Mouse King Christmas decoration that I'd given her mother when she was a child that helped decorate their living room during the holidays. Now all this sadness and worry was making sense.

"You don't have to be sad or afraid. Your mommie was a mouse one year in 'The Nutcracker.' It's all pretend. Just a show. So you don't have a thing to worry about. You can even be one of the mice yourself. You only *wear* a mouse costume—you don't really *become* a mouse. There's nothing to be afraid of. Those are fake swords and no one ever gets hurt."

She didn't miss a beat. "Lovie, can you come tuck me in?"

"Absolutely. Lovie will come tuck you in." Again.

Once in her bed Hayden said, "I want you to snuggle with me all night long. Never leave me. Let's snuggle…*all* night."

I thought about how unfair it might seem that her mother had her dad to snuggle with all night long. All Hayden had was stuffed animals, her books, and her Bumble Bee flashlight I'd given her for Christmas so she could find missing dolls in the dark, her favorite blanket her Grandmother Cee-Cee and PaPa had given her, and of course, Honey Bunny.

I whispered, "You know Hayden, when you are afraid and scared, you can always talk to God. He's always listening."

"But where is God? How can He hear us?"

Sleepy now, I hadn't counted on theological questions of this magnitude. Keep it simple, I thought. She's so young, keep it simple.

I said, "Well, Precious, God lives in heaven. And He sent His son Jesus to be with us for awhile…." She's too young, I thought. I can't give her details yet. Even her mother still feels an uncomfortable sensation in her hands and feet every time a picture of Jesus on the cross flashes onto the big screen in church. What happened to Jesus is so…unbearable. Oh God, I can't share that with her…yet.

That's when Hayden finished my answer for me, "Lovie, Jesus lives in our heart."

Relieved, I said, "That's right Baby Girl. Jesus lives in our heart. And He promises to never leave us. Ever. He snuggles with us always. And you can talk to Jesus too, when you're afraid because He's always with you and hears you every time you call."

With that last thought in her head, her fingers finally stopped pulling at Honey Bunny's loose string. Her body relaxed, jerked once, then the child finally drifted off into sandman land.

Later, after feeling a knee-stab to my ribs, I sneaked back into my bed and turned out the light, but not before I fluffed up the pillow that rested in Hayden's spot, for I knew snuggle bunnies were made to snuggle and would come hopping back to the nest when the moon was high and the stars were at their shiniest, most sparkly selves.

In fact, I could count on Hayden's and Honey Bunny's return, especially after I'd been so easily duped. This child wasn't afraid of anything, much less a mouse. She had an imagination that was bigger than the Pacific Ocean and her parents had shared the many ways *they* had been duped by this intelligent child before. So I fluffed up her pillow and waited for her and Honey Bunny to pay me another nocturnal visit.

I didn't have to wait long before I heard my door handle turn. "Haaaayyyyydennnn," I said before the child cut me off.

"But…Lovie…"

"Hayden, you and Honey Bunny come get in this bed right now." I patted the other side of the mattress. "I saved your spot. It's time to snuggle alllllll night."

Once she was safe in my arms, I whispered, "Je t'aime and Goodnight" and once again, her world was made right and she and her Lovie snuggled all night with Honey Bun.

But what would our defense be later when answering to her Mom and Dad about the broken rules? I could hear my excuses now: "Honey, remember that time you came to my room when you were five years old with every stuffed animal and baby doll you could carry because you could hear the frogs down at the pond and the cicadas and hoot owls outside your open window and you cried, 'The screaming eagles are going to carry off my *babies*!'?

"Well, kids, last night your daughter and I battled the Mouse King. She was simply fearless."

That was my story, and I was sticking to it because time is short. And there will come a time when my Grandees won't want to sleep in their Lovie's bed. So for now, I'm going to get in all the snuggles I can, because grandmothers need snuggle bunnies' snuggles too!

⚘ 18 ⚘
Cat Funerals

Jewel was a favorite cat. The last time seen, she was dead on the living room floor. When four-year-old Nicholas was asked by his sister if he'd seen the cat dead on the floor he replied, "No, the last time I saw her she was on the table."

Nick's sister planned the funeral. She scoured the back yard to find the finest rock to paint for a headstone. Of course, there would be a funeral service. Prayers needed to be said so Jewel could get into cat heaven since Jewel had never been saved or baptized. That was all a little fuzzy since it might be different for cats. How they got in. Maybe St. Peter kept a different book for animals and maybe there was a different way to get into heaven since cats hated anything to do with water whether it be a sprinkle, a dunk, or a pouring. They preferred dry washing and taking chances on hairballs, which were much more likely than meteor collisions. So maybe that was penance enough. However, Jewel's exploits would be remembered, at least for one day anyway.

When Nick showed up for the funeral and saw the tombstone at the head of the freshly dug mound of dirt with the name *Jewel* painted on in big bold letters, he pitched a hissy fit.

"What's the problem with the tombstone?" Nick's sister asked. "Jewel deserved to have something nice written about her. She was a good mouser!"

"It's my very favorite rock," wailed Nick. "And you've taken it and painted stuff all over it."

Nick screamed, cried, and vehemently protested. Nick had also been disruptive the year before at another cat's funeral when he'd come out during the service asking for puddin'.

His sister had said, "We're not messing with you and your puddin'. We're trying to have a cat funeral. Go away."

Nick ran into the house and found a container of puddin' and ran back outside. Without a spoon.

"You can't eat puddin' without a spoon," said Sister. So, Nick ran back inside, and later returned with a spoon. No one knew where he'd found the spoon or if the spoon was clean or if the spoon was dirty. But against all odds, Nick ate puddin' during the eulogy.

And now, Nick screamed, wailed and kicked out his frustration because Sister had found his special favorite rock in all the world and had desecrated it, all because of a cat.

Sister couldn't wait to call Great-Grandmother to tell her all about the latest cat funeral and how they'd eulogized Jewel. Great-Grandmother called Great-Aunt and told her she needed to get the family together and drive up from Florida to attend the next cat funeral.

Great-Aunt said, "I'm not driving all the way up to Tennessee to attend a cat funeral."

Great-Grandmother said, "Well, you might think about it, they serve puddin'."

Great-Aunt said, "Well, in that case, I might have to change my mind."

✧ 19 ✧
The Potholder

The first time I remember praying on my own was when I was a little girl. My family and I had summer plans to go to the lake for a swim and a picnic. Wearing a bathing suit with ruffles in the back, I also wore my colorful inner tube around my waist so I could float in the water without fear of drowning since I couldn't yet swim. While patiently waiting for family members to get ready for our outing, I was sitting on the living room sofa—the sky turning from blue to gray, when I heard Mother say, "It looks like it's going to rain. We may have to go to the lake another day."

When the raindrops began to fall, so did my child's beating heart. I began to pray. "God, I really want to go to the lake today, but if it rains, we can't go. Please stop the rain, God. Please stop the rain. I can't wait for another sunny day to swim."

Within about five minutes, the rain eased before totally stopping. Imagine how surprised I was, thinking God had answered a child's prayer. I was elated, just thinking that God would stop the rain for me. With one prayer. For one child. I treasured that special moment and never told one soul for fear I would be ridiculed.

Later, my wonderment about that rainy day would

subside. I realized that summer showers were sporadic and some stopped as quickly as they started. More than likely, what I'd experienced wasn't so special after all.

The incident no longer seemed as special, though I often wondered, *Did God really stop the rain for me?* He never answered in one way or another. So there were times I would forget about God. Times I would forget to pray until the next time I went back to church. It was hard for a little child to have a conversation with a God who didn't talk back when I talked to Him, and sometimes I forgot He even existed.

Until one day, I was outside sitting on my front porch making potholders. Someone had given me a metal loom with a bag of cotton loops and I had so much fun making potholders and giving them to my mother, family, and friends. I made yellow and green potholders. And potholders that were blue and red. Some I made were blue and yellow. When down to my last loops, I noticed all I had left were blue and green. And I thought a blue and green potholder would be the ugliest potholder ever made.

But then, my attention was suddenly drawn to the blue sky above. It was a gorgeous day with a few big fat fluffy clouds floating by—a day when bluebirds fly high and redbirds fluff their wings. As I looked at the sky, I noticed the green leaves of a tall tree and then lower, green grass that grew up to meet the azure. It was then I heard God whisper into my spirit, "See, blue and green do look good together. I made the grass and leaves green so the color would be a pleasant color that would be easy for the eyes to look at for long periods of time without tiring. And the blue of the sky where it touches the trees is such a soft blue, the color fades to gentle the greeting of the two colors when they meet."

It was then I knew without a doubt, I'd heard God's whisper. I could hear Him talking to me. Not in an audible voice. But somehow in my head and mind, somehow deep inside of me, He spoke to teach me. It was as though He'd cupped my chin and turned my face to look at the sky and trees as He shared with me about His beautiful creation. I would later learn that the still small whisper was God's Holy Spirit speaking to me.

And the blue and green potholder? I thought it so pretty I decided to give it to my Aunt Inez, an aunt who sometimes let me stay with her. An aunt who loved and cherished me and in the future would love my own children.

Many years later, after Aunt Inez had passed through the veil to return Home, I made another blue and green potholder. This one was for me. To be a constant reminder not only of God's blue skies and green leaves and grass—His creation— but also that I am a pot He's fashioned so the Holy Spirit can be my teacher and comforter while His Son Jesus is my savior, intercessor, and "holder" for eternity. The magnificent and awesome potholder of my soul. The Christ who helps me and holds me forever. He considers me His bride. He, the One and Only who will always cherish me and never let me go—even on rainy days.

"I, the Lord thy God, will hold thy right hand, saying unto thee, 'Fear not, I will help thee.'" Isaiah 41:13

~ 20 ~
From 14-Karat Mind to the Mind of Christ

Eleanor was the classiest lady I'd ever met. Gracious, loving, thoughtful, she was a mentor, to be sure, during my younger adult years. After childbearing, she'd managed to keep her youthful shape and always looked well put together and ready to take on the civilized world with a flick of a bejeweled wrist and well-manicured hand. Never a hair out of place.

I was looking forward to visiting with her once again.

After making my entrance into the hotel ballroom to attend a fashion show with several friends, I searched the tables to find my name card. There was Eleanor motioning to me and patting a seat beside her. "Vicki, so glad to see you. Sit next to me."

What an honor! I complemented Eleanor on her hair. Her jewelry. Her dress. Ahhhh. Yes. Her silk dress. She always sported a "finished" look of polish and perfection. Never a hair-wrinkle in a linen skirt. Never had I seen a lipstick smudge on her smooth cheeks. Her clothes, more than likely, were purchased in New York, San Francisco, London, Dallas, or Atlanta. Bedecked with jewelry, all of her jewelry "sets" were complete.

I was still waiting to get the ruby necklace that would match my ring. After that addition, perhaps I'd put a ruby bracelet on my wish list. Then maybe I'd try to finish out a sapphire set. Wouldn't emeralds be nice! And pearls. Every Southern girl had to have a bracelet to match her pearl necklace and earrings. Especially one with diamonds.

Maybe one day.

Then I remembered. "A big congratulations to you, Miss Eleanor, for making the Ten Best Dressed Women list. I only *dream* of making that list—ha-ha," I said. "Though it will take a lot of work and will be daunting, I'll have to try to follow in your footsteps."

Always humble, the virtuous and charitable woman beside me said, "Oh, Vicki, being voted onto that list and having my name in the newspaper has its downside. Now, every time I step out of my house, I feel I must always look perfect. I'm afraid not to dress to perfection for fear someone will say, 'How in the world did *she* ever make that list?' It's an honor to make the list, but truly, I don't like the scrutiny."

Surprised at this candid confession, I replied, "I never thought about it that way. Maybe you're right. Making the list sort of puts you under a magnifying glass, or it's similar to living in a glass house. Yes, maybe you're right. Perhaps I don't want to be on that list! I'm usually wearing blue jeans and flannel shirts. I refuse to dress up to go to the grocery store or the feed store. Some days I haul hay in the trunk of my car!"

"Exactly what I'm talking about," said Eleanor.

Hmmm. As other friends began to seat themselves next to us and the fashion show commenced, several beautiful and thin models sashayed down the runway. Watching them, I began thinking more about what Eleanor had said. Her words were pearls of wisdom. Once one made the Best Dressed list, I could only imagine the critics coming out of the woodwork in droves to see if the honored one could hold their place on the high pedestal.

I could hear them saying things about me.

"That outfit sure makes her look chunky."

"Someone as short as she is should certainly avoid horizontal stripes. What was she thinking?"

"Why did she ever in her wildest dreams think she could rock the color orange? Disaster the minute she stepped off the front step."

"Her hair is a mess today. Wonder who told her she could sport a ponytail. Makes her look so horsey and downright long in the tooth."

I could hardly eat the salad placed in front of me for thinking, *It would be extremely hard to muck out a barn without breaking a sweat and getting my jeans filthy. And that mission trip I'd gone on to Jamaica, the one where I had to hike a mile and a half down a mountain to get to church in hot, humid weather—my hair plastered to my damp scalp—then hike back up to the mission listening to the sounds of bleating goats, crowing roosters, and thinking about the moaning men who'd gotten into machete fights the night before, no glamorous moments there.*

Thank the Lord there were no photographers around to record those unflattering snapshots of me looking like a wilted magnolia blossom or a drooping peony flower pounded and walloped by a heavy rain. Let's just call it like it was—I was a sweaty mess. No reason to rewrite history.

I sighed as I waited for the chicken entrée to be set before me and watched the next pouty model purse her lips before making a well-heeled turn back to the dressing room and a fast change. And I kept dwelling on Eleanor's words, my not-so-fashion-flattering mission trip and my all-around casual life in general. There were certainly no silk dresses or fancy jewelry on *that* Caribbean trip.

The simple truth was, I enjoyed letting my hair down. A lot. I'd much rather be roasting hot dogs over an open fire down at the pond with my children listening to the whip-poor-wills calling to their mates than worrying if the linen I was wearing was beginning to look like a limp dishrag.

As I watched to see what icon of fashion finesse would next appear on the runway, I couldn't help but wonder if Eleanor had ever heard of Jesus Christ. Though she was Jewish, was she devout? Should I approach the subject? No. Best not go there. Wouldn't want to offend her and hurt our relationship. I'd best let God handle that subject.

A couple of years went by and I was notified of Eleanor's passing. Arriving late at the synagogue to pay my last respects, I discovered that almost everyone else had already left. A sad feeling fell over me like a final curtain made of wet, sagging velvet. There was more meaning behind my tears and I knew it. The loss was more than losing a treasured friend. I couldn't stop crying for this woman. Yet I couldn't quite explain my emotions to her surviving family.

Perhaps the copious tears had to do with my never

broaching the subject of the Messiah with her. That He'd already come and He'd died for her. I wondered if anyone had told her about Jesus before she breathed her last. I'd had a "religious" decision to make when it came to Eleanor…and I'd chosen to never broach the subject of Jesus. Is this why I couldn't stop sobbing?

Many more years would pass before I had to make another "religious" decision to speak up about Christ or stay silent. I recalled the verse from Matthew 10:33: *"Whosoever shall deny me before men, him will I also deny before my Father which is in heaven."*

I certainly didn't want to deny Christ, but I didn't want to offend anyone either. *Lord, there are better-equipped people to share the Gospel with those of other faiths. Please send someone else.*

When a friend of mine lost her son in a tragic death—a death by suicide from a river's bridge—I had to make a choice: Tell this grieving Indian woman of the Hindu faith about the only Son of God who could heal her emotional wounds and take a chance I might offend her, or keep silent. *Lord, help me here*, I cried out. *This woman is in agony and you know I'm not good at this witnessing to people about my own faith much less to those of other faiths. What should I do?*

Six months after the passing of my friend's son and after much prayer, I called this bereaved woman to invite her to dinner during the Christmas holidays. Before the appointed time, I searched the bookstore for a book I could wrap and give her for a Christmas present. A book about Jesus.

When the evening arrived, I gathered up a precious

woman still knee-deep in grief mire-mixed with anger because of the loss of her only son, and whisked her off to try to help ease her battle-scarred mind.

"I've never been out to dinner without my family," my friend shared.

Shocked at this revelation from a very modern-day and highly trained woman who held an important job in a professional field, I listened as she poured out her story. How a woman from her country was expected to marry someone of her parents' choosing. How there were never any "girls' night out" evenings with women friends. Ours was her first. How the tragedy of losing her son had rocked her world.

On the way home after an excellent dinner and much needed girl talk, I determined I was not going to have regrets concerning my cherished friend of the Hindu faith like the regrets I had with my Jewish friend, Eleanor.

Life is fragile. Either one of us could be killed in a car wreck on the morrow or be run down by a Mack truck while crossing the road, I surmised. Somehow, I would gather the courage to mention Jesus to the woman in the seat next to me and I would give her the book I had wrapped as a Christmas present, even though her family did not celebrate Christmas and the birth of Christ.

Oh Lord, please give me the courage to speak lovingly but boldly. I don't want to offend and hurt this woman anymore than she has already been hurt. I know I'm supposed to have the mind of Christ, but frankly, I fall so short when it comes to being Christ-like.

Before my friend got out of the car, I gave her the gift. As she unwrapped the book, I explained to her that the reading material was about Jesus, the only Son of God. The one who claimed so many years ago, *"I am the way, the truth, and the life: no man cometh unto the Father, but by me"* John 14:6, and suggested perhaps Jesus would heal her hurts like He'd healed so many of mine if she gave Him a chance and called on Him to help her.

My dear friend immediately began to share with me about her 30,000 gods. I was semi-literate about her 30,000 gods and the Hindu belief that humans were reincarnated and kept coming back to relive life on earth until they "get it right"... or something along those lines. Frankly, I stopped studying about Eastern religions when I shuddered to think that if I was reincarnated, there was a possibility I could come back as a rat, which was so repulsive to me that I was even more convinced Jesus was the real deal, though I'd never had a doubt at that point in my life that Jesus had to be the only way. He was who He claimed to be. When my dear friend finished trying to enlighten me, however, I thanked her for sharing, and we hugged goodbye.

On the way home, I prayed, "Lord, I've done what I feel you would have wanted me to do. I have introduced my friend—the wonderful person our Father created—to you and I place her salvation solely in your hands and pray the Holy Spirit will eventually stir her heart so she will come to know you and the Father like I know you."

The rest of the story? I'm still waiting for the "She lived happily ever after story ending. That phone call—the one where my friend says, "I've found Jesus and have made Him my Lord and Savior so I will live eternally!" So far, I haven't heard those words from her. I know, however, that all is in God's timing and my prayers are being heard. But there is one good thing that has come out of my sharing about the Messiah to those of different faiths: I no longer have a 14-Karat mind. I quickly came to the realization that Jesus is right, my earthly treasures can't go to heaven with me. There are more important things to do on earth while here than polishing silver and longing after gold and adding to "collections."

I'm working every day to be more Christ-like, striving to have a mind like Christ because I want no more regrets. And I'm going to repeat this verse often: *Who hath known the mind of the Lord, that he may instruct him? But we have the mind of Christ.* 1 Corinthians 2:16

Besides, the walls of the New Jerusalem—the heavenly city where I'll be living when not hanging out in the heavenly barn—are built on foundations made of sapphires and every kind of jewel including emeralds, and the streets are paved with gold. I will have no need for "matching jewelry sets" or silk dresses or wrinkling linen. I'll be arrayed wearing "garments of salvation" and "robes of righteousness." Who could ask for more?

~ 21 ~
I Could Have Been a Contender if I Hadn't Had a Jesus Crush

Yep. Did it. Wrote about the time I wore a red jumpsuit and sashayed into a pop star's concert. Front row seats.

Toted binoculars. I was there to ogle this sexy gyrating star busting a move. I thought he was the greatest dancer who'd ever lived. He could shake a leg better than Elvis.

Years later, when I began writing, I wrote about the event for a writing contest. All in jest. I didn't have to embellish too much while keeping the story within the confines of creative nonfiction. It is true, however, that the star bumped and grinded all the way over to my side of the stage and that my friend leaned over and said, "He's singing to you" and I replied "Yes, I know," without taking my eyes off the idol.

I entered that story in a humor contest, wondering if my humor was funny enough to place. What, exactly, did it take to write humor, which was considered difficult by many? After the contest, I intended to give the story a quick burial. I was not particularly proud of this story. Well, maybe I was, because it *was* pretty funny. This contest was for a secular conference and before God had totally convinced me I needed to be writing for Him.

The humor judge was the same woman critiquing our manuscripts.

She said, "You have to take out, 'That was before my to-think-it-in-your-heart-is-the-same-as-committing-the-sin days.' Sounds like a Jimmy Carter statement."

"I can't take that sentence out. My entire story hinges on that one line!"

"Well," she said, "people won't laugh. And, you need to take out 'Priapus worshippers.' Your readers are rednecks. They won't get it. *I* don't know what that means."

Like, c'mon. Rednecks don't own a dictionary or know how to Google? Let 'em do some research and find out why God was so angry in the Old Testament.

After she'd cut it down to newspaper column length, she shoved it at me. "Read this on open mic night."

Horrified, I said, "I can't read that out loud—*In Public*!"

"Oh, c'mon."

Well, from her pressuring me to read it, maybe she liked it a little. Maybe it had an honorable-mention chance.

But what about my reputation? I'd be labeled "Scarlet Woman."

I lost sleep. Tossed and turned for most of the night.

Prayed.

After God let me suffer through 1,000 imaginary upside down crucifixions with added fire, in the stillness of the early morning I heard in my heart, "Go ahead. Read it. I'll turn it around for good. Later, you can witness about how you love Jesus."

My voice quivered as I said, "God, that had better be you."

With fear and trembling I wore red. Swiped on matching lipstick for a visual.

Ratcheting up courage, I stepped to the mic, feeling like Miss Melanie on the inside, looking like Miss Scarlet on the outside, I stood before God and a redneck audience—according to the contest judge—reminiscing about lusting after a pop star in skin-tight pants.

Surprised myself.

Belted out lyrics. "Whoa, whoa, whoa."

Said, "I looked hot.

"I was hot."

(Like one writer friend once said, "Well, we were all hot back then!")

But my daughter later said, "Mom, I can't believe you wrote that!" She was mortified.

I replied, "Darlin', I was young once and wore a size four before you came along and wrecked my miry temple of clay."

Okay, I'm digressing to keep from telling the worst part. But here's the rest of the story. After I saw the "star" kissing all of those women carrying Champagne bottles and long-stemmed roses up to the stage for a lip-lock, I thought, Gross! No way was I going to be lured to the spotlight and swap spit with all of those lusting women. Where, in that idol's lifetime, had those sweet lips been? A bulldozer couldn't have pried me off my seat for a kiss even if they'd paid me.

Then here's what happened later at open mic nite.

While I was reading my story, laughter tinkled in all the right places.

If the rednecks didn't know what some of the words meant, they laughed anyway, went home and looked up the words, and learned why God hates idols. And when I talked about "that was before my to-think-it-in-your-heart-is-the-same-as-committing-the-sin days," my audience laughed there too. I figured they all must have voted for Jimmy Carter and bought his books, or perhaps they were laughing at him, and not with him, which wasn't very nice either.

But I lived through that travesty without God calling down lightning to strike me dead or sending in a horde of toads. So I figured that was truly God I heard from the night before, though I was kinda peeved at Him for letting me wrestle with my dilemma and lose sleep 'til two in the morning.

The next day, during lunch break at the conference, I strolled to the lunch room, went through the line for red snapper, and set my tray down on a table. There was a guy already there and I could see his name on his name tag. Being friendly, I introduced myself. With no hint of laughter in his voice, but with humorous undertone and twinkling eyes, he replied, "Oh, I know who you are." Long pause. "And I will *never* forget you."

He wore a long ponytail. Looked like the literary type. It could have been he was there incognito as a redneck. I refrained from pulling back his collar to check because I didn't want him checking mine. Who was I kidding? He already knew the color of *my* neck after open mic nite. He'd obviously been there to witness my confession of the night before.

I glanced at a couple of Rome acquaintances sitting at the next table over—not the Rome across the big pond but the Rome south of the little pond below Tennessee and east of Alabama. I let out an embarrassed laugh. A nervous laugh. A where-do-you-want-a-door-in-that-wall-because-I'm-getting-ready-to-make-one laugh.

Everybody else laughed *hearty* laughs. Glad-it-was-you-instead-of-me laughs. My face flamed blue it was so red hot, and I asked those within shouting distance, "Have you not ever done anything stupid in your younger days?"

Harmonizing, the Georgia Peach girls quipped, "Well *yeah*, but we don't *talk* about it!"

Desperate for approval and trying to save myself, I said, "Do you still love me now you know I lusted?"

The peaches sang out acapella, "Only 'cause Jesus tells us to!"

A big, toothy-grinned guy said, "That was a great story you read last night! You had me blushing and chuckling. I'd heard about women being aggressive these days. I didn't know how far you were gonna take that!" He invited me to move into his new resort community on the coastal waters of the Atlantic. Invited me to go with him to cast line. He could have been a fishing pervert. One never knew. (Turned out he was happily married and only trying to sell real estate lots in a coastal neighborhood. Whew!)

I said, "Remember Hoss, it's *creative* nonfiction. The entire story hinged on that one line: that was before I knew to-think-it-in-my-heart-was-the-same-as-sinning days.

I kept thinking, *God, I can't believe you encouraged me to act like a fool—oh yeah, you put Jeremiah through the wringer too. Anyway Lord, I will never live this down.*

At the end of the conference on awards night, as the honorable mention was called, I was disappointed because my story hadn't won that. It didn't even take third. Then it didn't take second. I'd acted an idiot for…*practice?*

Then, I heard my name.

Whoa, whoa, whoa!

And yes, the scarlet woman wore red down the carpet to accept her first place award for "I Could Have Been a Contender."

But that wasn't the end of the story. I later wrote another story, about writing the first story, which became "My Redneck Summer"…which also won first place—in an international contest. And I've used these stories to speak to many people about Christ and how most of us have done stupid things in our youth before we matured and dove deeper into God's word.

God did indeed do as He'd promised that night of my tossing and turning. He turned my foolishness around for good. *We know that all things work together for good to them that love God, to them who are the called according to his purpose.* Romans 8:28

The rest of the story: I still have the red jumpsuit, but only to remind people of my stupidity. My daughter even loaned it to one of her few girlfriends who could squeeze into a size four and she wore it to an 80s party. And all of her friends heard about my pop idol story and the writing contest and my "winning" performance. Isn't it amazing how God can really turn a sow's ear into a silk purse and everything works out to glorify and honor Him?

I now pray Psalm 25:7 without ceasing: *Remember not the sins of my youth, nor my transgressions: according to thy mercy remember thou me for thy goodness' sake, O LORD.*

~ 22 ~
If Only by Toe-Touch

On a bone-marrow-freezing February day, I, a slim 12-year-old girl who almost died of Bright's Disease when I was seven and had to miss a year of school in the 1930s, heard Daddy say, 'The boy's gone to hook up the mules to pull us out so we can get to the chapel.' And within 30 minutes, there was the 14-year-old neighbor who lived in our cove driving Maude and Mandy down the slick rutted-out road, ready to hook up to the bumper of Daddy's Model-T that was stuck hub deep in brown mud.

"Peering out the back window, a hand resting on my seven-month-old baby brother's tiny casket that had been placed on the back seat between my sister—who was two years younger—and me, I never took my gaze off the wiry young boy with black hair who talked and clucked to his already overworked yet obedient mules. That day…was the day…I fell in love with your Daddy. And never stopped loving him."

"But I wasn't in love with your Mother," Daddy said, ears wiggling while his laughter filled the family room. "I thought she was too young for me back then. And when I received a letter during the war overseas from the cove in Alabama, a letter that was from her, I never answered her back."

"Can you believe that?" Mother added incredulously.

The room filled with more laughter and disbelief as the fire crackled and popped in my parents' mountaintop home.

"Wasn't it good to get news from home?" I asked Daddy. Mother had always taught me to answer letters and to write thank you notes.

"Yes, it was good to get news from home," Dad replied. "The boys I soldiered with during World War II were always hungry for news. But I wasn't the best letter writer and was living in foxholes most of the time, jumping as a paratrooper behind enemy lines, and didn't take the time to write my own family often, much less shy little girls. I was dodging bullets and sometimes I fought while sick with spine-rattling flu. Everything in me ached. The doctors were ordered to give us an aspirin and send us back to the front lines. We were short on men and fearful the enemy would break through our lines. And we sometimes lived in five feet of snow in forests crawling with the enemy. So back to the front lines and my foxhole I went.

"When I was off duty during a lull or when our commanding officers pulled us off the front line and shipped us back to England for a rest before the big push to end the war, I was interested in having fun dating the English girls more my age. I didn't think much about the girls back home. I lived for the moment because I might die in the next battle."

When Daddy arrived stateside, having survived four hellacious years in the European theatre fighting Hitler's war—with all but about five of the 125 men in his original Company I, either buried in Europe or sent to other commands because of ankle and leg injuries from bad landing falls—he was bone thin, battle weary, and suffering from combat fatigue and nightmares. Back then, the term Post Traumatic Stress Disorder (PTSD) had yet to be coined.

One thing Daddy knew—"I wanted to settle down and marry and have a family. I was tired of killing. I was tired of waking up at night reliving battles, dangerous river crossings, and beachhead landings where I lost some of my best men. I wanted to move forward with my life. I wanted to live.

"My family had moved to the city before I joined the Army but first thing I did when I arrived home from Germany was buy a car so I could drive back to the cove to visit the old folks and to ask about your mother's younger sister by a couple of years. She wasn't as shy as your mother. I was told she'd married. So I asked about your mother—I thought the world of her family—and was told she had moved to town as well, to find work in a drugstore."

Mother picked up the story from there. "I was painfully shy. A straight A student but too shy to read an English paper in front of the class in high school. When the teacher asked me to read my work, I declined. The teacher said, 'You can read your "A" paper to the class or take an "F."' I could barely be heard when I whispered with downcast eyes, 'I'll take the "F."'

"Of course the teacher didn't give me the bad grade. He was only trying to pull me out of my shell. So one day, about five years later when the war had ended, when I looked up to see your daddy walking down the aisle of the drugstore wearing his uniform, I couldn't believe my eyes. The boy I'd always dreamed about had returned home. And he had come to look me up—even though I was his second choice because I was the shy sister! We were married within two months. It took me a few years to become more outgoing, but I finally decided being shy was no fun—and eventually did venture from my shell. Your Daddy was the only man for me.

"And I finally got the boy I saw through the back window of our Model T Ford on that frozen-ground day when the only flowers blooming for a funeral were yellow jonquils that had managed to pop open in spite of the cold weather. Even though I'd lost one of the loves of my life—my little brother who was like my own child and the sweetest and happiest baby—and was on my way to his funeral, I'd found another love."

"The rest is history," Daddy said. "I flew back to the States after Germany surrendered and the Russian army poured in, your Mother and I had you three children, and here we are… still married like two peas in a pod."

But even I, despite all this lovey-dovey talk, knew my parents' marriage hadn't always been easy…as hardly any marriages are, if couples are truthful. So Mother shared one last important tidbit, "Even though we might have had the biggest argument during the day, our feet always touched at night when we slipped beneath the covers—even during the most hot and humid nights. We never stopped being close to one another, if only by toe-touch beneath the sheets."

An amazingly true two-peas-in-a-pod toe-touch love story.

But perhaps there was more. I'd often wondered about those two lovebirds. Mother almost dying from a disease most never recovered from back then when doctors lived across the way beyond raging rivers that had yet to be tamed, and during a time when medicines were hard to find…if there was any money to be had during the depression.

And then there was Daddy. Wounded once to receive a purple heart along with several other medals. He shouldn't have survived World War II when many paratroopers were killed in the sky—"sitting ducks" before landing—and others were taken out by land mines and hidden machine gun nests. Daddy was frequently behind enemy lines or on the front lines facing tanks that tried to blow men from their foxholes, or planes that strafed mountain-high tactical positions that were so steep the wounded, bloodied, and broken, had to be tied to rocks to keep from rolling down Italy's mountains before medics could arrive with stretchers during a lull in battle.

But somehow, for some reason, Daddy did survive when so many others failed to live to make it home.

And then years later, against all odds, I was born, the third child to a man who wanted only two children. When this realization finally dawned on me, that technically or by wishful thinking, I shouldn't have been born, I had an awakening. My soul and spirit had beaten several odds to make an appearance in the form of a human being, a body of clay, a temple for the Holy Spirit. And I could only deduce that I was here by God's grace, writing for Him, telling tall tales and a few short ones, for a reason—acknowledging to others my life had meaning.

Yes, I'm here for a grander purpose in life, to glorify God with my writing and my life's testimony. Perhaps for my descendants. Perhaps for others who do not yet know Christ. And perhaps to bolster Christians who are world-weary and need to hear about the stories of others while also striving to walk in the light, no matter how difficult the journey.

I only pray, that having survived this cruel world so far, I do God and the story of His Only Son justice as He guides me through this life of many trials. That I tell the stories that need to be told, humbly and truthfully, and in such a way that God's Word will come alive so others may seek Christ to know Him; to live eternally.

And I pray I never forget God's calling and Isaiah 43:7: *[Even] every one that is called by my name: for I have created him for my glory, I have formed him; yea, I have made him.*

And that if my parents lived through horrendous atrocities and both experienced near death to "accidentally" bring me into such a wicked world full of sinful people who would persecute God's chosen ones, I must remember that *whether therefore ye eat, or drink, or whatsoever ye do, do all to the glory of God.* 1 Corinthians 10:31

Therefore, know this: We are *all* here for a purpose. And I will continue to pray that those who read the Moments' book series, where many of my stories were first published, will be encouraged to seek their purpose in life as well.

May God bless, and always be with you as you seek your higher calling and a closer relationship with the Lord. And may you always toe-touch with your loved one beneath the covers—until death do you part and God calls you home.

❧ 23 ❧
A Day for Me

Finally, my day for a haircut, pedicure, and mani. A day just for me...to relax, unwind, and indulge myself. Per usual, the beautiful soul inside and out—who also cuts my hair—will chat with me and share about deep and meaningful things.

Sometimes we chat about how COVID nearly did us both in. How she felt Jesus holding her hand after she'd prayed for the Lord to heal her. How she almost died and it took her eight weeks to recover.

I share with her about begging Jesus to take me because I felt like I wanted to die if I didn't get released from the hospital soon. After five days, I was still weak. I felt I would surely die if I had to stay in there another day.

Then, I share with her about my home invasion and how life is sometimes too much. Overwhelming. But as always, God sees and carries us through.

We strengthen each other talking about our faith and I leave bolstered and ready to keep going forward in this crazy world. Jesus might have more work for me to do.

Then I go to get my mani and pedi and Justin (not his real name)—the new guy who does my nails—tells me his wife cheated on him. He uses a translator app on his phone and then shows it to me because I can't understand much of what he says. He knew the English word "cocaine," and could make the pew pew sound and hand gesture. He showed me a video of his wife meeting up with his best friend, who happens to be a cocaine dealer and has been meeting her at a seedy motel. In the video, the guy comes out, waves what looks like either a "Judge" or perhaps another type of pistol and threatens to kill Justin. Justin's wife comes into the picture and goes into the motel room and shuts the door.

Surreal. Like I'm getting ready to watch the gunfight at the OK Corral. I'm seeing someone's marriage fall apart in a real time movie. On a phone. While getting my nails filed and polished. Maybe Justin's wife later left the motel. The conversation happens fast, however, I get the gist of things. Justin tells me his court date is in April. I ask if he has an interpreter to take with him.

"Yes. Divorce cost me $6,000."

He talks into his phone so the conversation will be translated into English for me. I read from the screen: "My best friend's wife is staying with her husband still, but my wife wants a divorce. We have a beautiful daughter who is two years old." He shows me her photo.

A total doll baby. I ask him if he's a Christian and he doesn't understand what I'm asking so he holds his phone up so I can speak into it and I say, "Are you a Christian?"

Thinking the phone didn't hear me, I say "Christian" louder. Everyone stares at us. I duck my head and ignore the stares. The words pop up on the screen in a foreign language. Justin looks at my words and says, "Him. But not me." Oh no. The man breaking up his marriage is a Christian. Not a good way to win someone to Christ. God hates adultery.

I don't feel like I can get into a conversation at this moment to tell Justin about the Gospel and how to be saved—I don't want to get him fired. However, he's going to need help to get through the next several years. He is asking for a 50/50 split, which he will get in Tennessee. I think about giving him money to help with his legal fees. Should I open up my purse and hand over some dollars? Whatever I have with me usually varies. Sometimes I carry no cash.

Then I begin wondering if I am being played. Plus, I don't want those around me to know I have cash on me. Who can be trusted these days?

Perhaps this is all a ruse. Perhaps Justin has a slick new trick to get older women to feel sorry for him. Play dumb. Get folks to hand him money. Panhandle the gullible.

I thought Justin's people were normally family-oriented and didn't go through such foolishness as adulterous affairs. I mean, how could this bad guy who happened to be a dear friend who came to visit every Friday night, steal away Justin's wife? Drugs are a powerful thing. But is Justin into drugs as well?

How could he not have known that his best friend is a drug dealer? Is Justin a dealer too? I choose not to leave cash, but leave the usual tip on my credit card.

Something seems off. Justin seems too happy. Most people in that situation would have a sad appearance. Downcast demeanor. Forlorn countenance. Now that I think about it more, Justin seems too happy-go-lucky. Too carefree. But his actions could be because he is desperately trying to keep himself sane, and maybe the only way he can do that is by sharing his dilemma with a total stranger. But why is he sharing all of this tragedy, if it is one, with *me*? Am I that random stranger he can vent to? Or is Justin on drugs himself?

Normally, as I stated before, I would give financially to help someone in dire straits. But after finding out some of the people I'd hired to help with home projects were from a country that had a reputation for being one of the worst countries for gangs and crime in the past, and that an art framing business in town was a front for illicit drugs —and with all of the unvetted people flooding into the country, I have become uneasy due to the uptick in violent crimes and theft in our area. I have become leery. More cautious.

All I can bring myself to do is silently pray.

"This time Lord, I'm leaving everything in your hands. It's impossible for me to share anything about You with him since he's working. I don't want to get him fired. Justin is God's creation. All I can do is pray for him and his situation. His future outcome is in Your hands. May your Holy Spirit guide and direct him. And may Your will be done in this tragic situation. Have mercy on his soul. Protect his beautiful child. And if it's for the best, turn his wife's heart back to him. Only *You* know the true story. Only *You* can help this man. In Jesus name I pray, Amen."

~ 24 ~
Searching for the Lost

My dear Mother used to hide some of her possessions from her children to keep us from using them. Scissors and pinking shears for instance. She didn't want children dulling the blades with paper because dull blades chewed fabric when trying to make garments. Then she couldn't recall where she'd hidden the scissors and pinking shears and they stayed lost for months. Searching for Mother's scissors made me vow I'd never lose things when I grew up.

That's laughable now. Because after I had a child of my own—when the sperm hits the egg the brain turns to mush—I couldn't recall where I'd put anything or even where I might have possibly lost something. I was especially unfortunate when it came to losing jewelry. I lost a bracelet while shopping in Oxford, Mississippi once and retraced my steps around the town square several times, inquiring in every store about my lost treasure. After searching dressing rooms I'd been in, concrete sidewalk cracks, and patches of well manicured grass, I finally gave up and darkened the door of The City Grocery restaurant to put some salve on my wound by forking shrimp and grits onto my taste buds. However, not even shrimp and grits could ease the pain of that bracelet loss.

Then there's my ongoing issue I have with the verse that

says that as a follower of Christ, I "have the mind of Christ." If I have the mind of Christ (who is omniscient and omnipresent), then Jesus, please show me where I lost that bracelet.

Nothing.

And recently, I misplaced a special ring. A favorite ring I'd worn for years. I remember telling myself I needed to put it in a better hiding place because I know thieves do break in; but like Mother with her scissors and pinking shears, I couldn't recall where the "better" place was. I searched high. Then low. Then all around. In cubbies. In corners. I searched everywhere for that elusive ring and could not find it.

Then I heard as plain as day in my spirit, "Would you search as hard for me as you are searching for that ring?" Aghast, I replied, "You know I would, Lord! Where did that even come from? You know I love you and have been seeking you ever since I was six years old. Studying your Word. Praying. Bullet prayers while in the car driving. How could you even ask that? Have I not been a servant? Well, most of the time? *Some* of the time?"

But another thought instantly popped into my head and the thought pained me more than the lost ring. *Well, if I'm ultra honest, I have gotten slack with my prayers lately. It's so easy to simply say, "Lord, bless the entire world, bring everyone to Christ so all can go to heaven. You know what everyone needs, especially heal the sick, and take care of the little ones. Turn the bad guys into good guys. Bless us all indeed, ditto the prayer I said yesterday, and Amen."*

And there's that pain I get when I kneel—do I have to bend the knee every time when I pray before bed? Yes, I know it helps me focus better when I'm on my knees but you know how my face starts itching and all I want to do is scratch.

No answer.

I then I thought about how I was praying. I wasn't thanking and praising enough. There were times when I was so hungry I wolfed down my food before even remembering I had forgotten to bless my food and pray a prayer of thanks, then felt guilty for not remembering to pray because I was thinking about my stomach more than I was thinking about my job down here on earth.

Am I not praying long enough? Eloquently enough? Not using the correct phraseology because I'm not using your favorite Bible translation? What is my exact job down here on my patch of ground anyway? This place is so hard to figure out. Don't pass go. Do pass go. *Okay, Lord, I'll try to do better. And I have been searching for you diligently, but it's really difficult when I can't look at you—have you seated in front of me over breakfast coffee and Irish tea. You get that You not being visible causes so many to backslide. I'm only human. I can't be the only filthy rag down here who is derelict in earthly duties. And yes, I'm aware there are a ton of lost people around me. But I'm just one person. What more would you have me do? Can you send me an email and lay it all out for me? Bullet points on a month-by-month calendar would help tremendously. A newsletter would be nice.*

And then, I feel like He's just—gone. And I'm left alone again to figure everything out by myself it seems.

How quickly my mind started to wander! On writing, for heaven's sake. I think I've written down every Christmas story

I can ever write. What else could I ever write about Christmas? Why did that even pop into my ever-loving mind?

Then I heard in my spirit: Christmas Tree Skirt. *Aha! Lord, you're still here. And yes, I haven't ever written about the Christmas tree skirt I made decades ago. Just when I thought you were no longer with me, you give me another great idea. When will I learn that your Word is a living Word?*

Nothing. Once again. But that one idea is enough. And that's the way I'm supposed to live. One step at a time it seems. For now.

And who knows, maybe, eventually, I'll be told where that favorite lost ring is while I'm searching for the lost.

Luke 15:9-10: *When she hath found it, she calleth her friends and her neighbors together, saying, 'Rejoice with me; for I have found the piece which I had lost.' Likewise, I say unto you, there is joy in the presence of the angels of God over one sinner that repenteth.*

≈ 25 ≈
Broken with Character

Broken. One meaning of the word is: violently separated into parts. My coccyx—or tailbone—has been broken three times. Though it probably didn't violently separate, I felt it had. Twice, from various 4-wheeler and dirt bike accidents. But the third time was the most humiliating accident and could have been prevented if my children and their friends had obeyed and played quietly in the barn. Instead, one little girl thought it would be funny to jump out from *behind* the barn, spooking the skittish young green horse I rode.

Totally unprepared for my daughter's friend's surprise joke—I was unseated as the horse jumped out from beneath me flying sideways while daylight winked for a couple of seconds between the ground and me before Mother Earth body slammed my spine.

Every time my coccyx fractured, it took a good two to three months for the pain to dissipate. Lifting a leg to climb stairs was the worst experience ever with an ailing tailbone.

I had trouble getting my breath back for what seemed like forever while I lay staring at passing clouds from the unforgiving ground. Luckily my back wasn't broken when that horse parted ways with my seat, and lucky for the visiting child, I was the forgiving type.

Did that unfortunate incident keep me from having unruly children over to visit?

No. They kept getting invited. And they kept coming.

I kept trying to mentor, if needed, and be there for my children's friends and for the children belonging to strangers from different states and countries that I welcomed into my home; even the almost-grown kiddos—one who broke my diving board trying to water the back 40—the same child someone back home loved. And also the one skinny rascal who jumped off my foyer balcony, sliding down a column onto the floor while holding an opened beverage. Boys will be boys. They say.

Recently, I had the opportunity to remember those youthful times during a requested afternoon tea party with my granddarlings. Why not bring out the paper-thin Belleek china for a three-year-old so she could enjoy tea with her five-year-old sister. What I hadn't counted on was her being overly enthusiastic when stirring in sugar to suit her taste. And that the china truly was paper-thin. Oh well, just one good little chunk missing right above the handle. Who would notice?

While washing up the tea cups and saucers that I'd purchased in Ireland many moons ago, I recalled Mother (a mom who'd had all of her cherished living room vases broken and glued back together before she returned home so she wouldn't notice) once saying, "People are what's important. Not things."

Her most famous words: "The fireplace soot will wash right out of those clothes," when I would say, "Do my children have to look like they've been playing in the fireplace ashes when I come to pick them up?" Mother simply laughed and proceeded to tell me how much fun they'd had singing and playing using the stone fireplace ledge as their stage.

Mother was notorious for saying, "Oh, I don't mind if they play with that—if it breaks we'll glue it back together," about her precious things. Then she'd tell me how the flour from the biscuit dough flew into the air when she was teaching them how to make biscuits. Or when they were older, how well they'd done sewing buttons on scrap material or how they'd made homemade lye soap in a huge cauldron over a fire outside. Mother was always one to teach a history lesson with hands-on activities. She insisted my girls learn Foxfire skills, things that were originally "down-home chores."

Watching the joy Mother experienced when hosting her annual cousin's breakfast, or July Fourth family celebration, or quilting bee, (or you name her event) was a blast because whatever she hosted, she came to her party with zeal and passion and a love for people. Even though she might have scooted her bottom through Daddy's vegetable garden, dragging her broken leg with its cumbersome cast behind her to gather her harvest, she rarely let something like a broken leg hold her down and continued planning the next big event.

And that was the kind of grandmother—one with zeal and passion for learning and life—I wanted to be for my grandees.

"Oh Harper…you broke my best china I use for tea, you little darling you. Oh well, what's a chip out of a tea cup!" Her older sister Hayden said, "Lovie, it's like Chip the teacup in *Beauty and the Beast*!"

"And that broken part will make this teacup special," I replied, winking at the darlings.

Forever after, that teacup would no longer be called Irish Belleek, but Chip. And at last, that teacup had some character while the granddarlings and I sang and danced to, "Be our guest, be our guest, put our service to the test...."

The lesson in fractured tailbones, clothes blackened from ashes, and broken tea cups is that there will always be brokenness in this life due to trials and testings. Jesus gave us a heads-up about that fact.

As long as we're in God's will, somehow, someway, the brokenness will all be worked out, whether it be a bone, a tea cup, or a black trial. In John 16:33, Jesus said, *"These things I have spoken unto you, that in me ye might have peace. In the world ye shall have tribulation: but be of good cheer; I have overcome the world."*

Paul gave us a piece of advice as well in Romans 8:28: *We know that all things work together for good to them that love God, to them who are called according to his purpose.*

Broken or not, messed up or not, God can use everyone. I agree with well-known missionary W.E.S. Holland who said, "Only he whose will is continually broken in the valley of humiliation can experience the joy of victory in Christ."

So, more and more I'm not overly worried about a few dirty clothes, broken china, and broken tailbone incidences—although they're no fun—nor am I bothered by a broken tea cup as long as the chip isn't in an area that could be dangerous to sensitive lips. But I must admit, I'm still working on enjoying being broken in the valley of humiliation.

Every time I reach a low place in that valley, though, I

know the rise to the hilltop is nigh. And I await the next new valley not with fear and trembling, but almost like waiting on an assignment for a new adventure. Anticipating where the journey will lead. And how my inevitable brokenness will somehow be turned into good to somehow further God's purposes. That's how I intend to live through my brokenness—with character—while putting my service to the test to try and be my best.

~ 26 ~
A Pinch Of Clay

A special creative time in my life was when I took a pottery class with Suzanne, a close and dear friend. It was in this class that I learned to throw a lump of clay onto a wheel to try to make it into something useful, and hopefully exquisite— either a bowl, cup, or vase. When I think back on the process, the step I enjoyed the most was pinching off a piece of clay from my allotted lump, throwing it on the wheel, and then centering the clay. If the clay wasn't centered, good luck with trying to place my thumbs in the middle of the clay to make a hole, to then squeeze the sides with wet fingers, pulling the clay up to make anything, for the clay would be one wobbly, ugly mess. But once that clay was centered, I loved cupping the lump of wet clay with my hands as it spun around on the wheel for a couple of minutes, reveling in the fact that for now my centered lump of clay was at its ultimate best as far as lumps go.

Trust me when I say this, the final culmination of the clay-centering process thrilled me. And this thrill was the big enchilada— in my playbook, the biggest high and eureka moment for a potter. Who knew you could rejoice over a centered lump of clay? If only a human life could be like that lump of clay, perfectly centered with its Creator, always.

Eventually, I had to rouse myself from my lump-centered reverie and make the holes in the center of the clay with my thumbs, to pull the sides of the clay up to get on with the work at hand: creating my masterpiece. As the sides of my lump stretched taller, things could get tricky in a heartbeat. If my hands and fingers weren't placed just right—and if I didn't hold my mouth just right—the project could go all wonky.

When I was first learning how to throw pots, that happened often. Now it was happening again. Oops! No worries. Not totally wrecked, I could make a few artistic dimples in the sides with my fingers, fire the piece, add a green glaze, and once my creation was completed it would look like the individual piece had been intentionally created to look "artistic." That was my story and I was sticking to it. Now on to the finish line.

When it was time to take my wire and pull it through the base of the vase to release it from the wheel, my wire broke through the bottom of the clay leaving a hole the size of a quarter. Oh no! I realized I had pushed too far down with my thumbs, not leaving enough thickness at the bottom of the vase. Rats! I decided to fire the piece in the kiln anyway, give it that beautiful green glaze, and put the "artwork" on a bookshelf at home because I liked the wonky looking vase. And, I reasoned, if I wanted to plant something in the vase, it now had a drainage hole! All I had to do was put a few rocks in the bottom to cover up the hole, add soil and a plant, and any excess water could drain through the soil, seep between the rocks and exit out the hole. So the vase was still functional and worth something other than being a thing of spectacular beauty—at least to me—and was a keeper. Plus, for some odd reason I could not fathom, I was simply attached to this unusual looking vase.

After pottery classes and a couple of years later, I was asked to teach a children's class in Vacation Bible School. But what would I teach? I began to have a one-sided conversation with God about this dilemma. Shortly thereafter, I was walking through my home on the way to the kitchen and my attention was drawn to an out-of-the-way bookshelf.

It was as if God had turned my head in that direction. I spotted that green vase I'd made years before, the one with the hole that had been broken through at the bottom, and I immediately knew what illustration I would use for the children's class—the story from Jeremiah 18:1-23. *"The word which came to Jeremiah from the Lord saying, 'Arise, and go down to the potter's house, and there I will let you hear my words.' So I went down to the potter's house, and behold, he wrought a work on the wheels. And the vessel that he made of clay was marred in the hand of the potter: so he made it again another vessel, as seemed good to the potter to make it."*

I thought about my wonky vessel that had been broken through at the bottom being cut from the wheel and how I'd "reworked" it into something functional and oddly beautiful. Then I was suddenly reminded of humanity and the condition of the human race. How we can be perfectly formed coming out of our mother's womb but when separated from the life-giving womb, life experiences can have their way of breaking us, sometimes physically and emotionally. But even though broken, after we make many mistakes and take wrong turns on our path of life, God can still redeem us and use us for His purposes. Even after we think we are no longer "usable" or fit for His work. As Romans 8:28 reminds us, God can turn anything into something good.

So the wonky looking vase with its brokenness, something the kids could see and touch, would be perfect to use as an illustration for the children's class. I then looked up other "clay pot" verses and Lamentations 4:2 caught my eye: *The precious sons of Zion, comparable to fine gold, how are they esteemed as earthen pitchers, the work of the hands of the potter!*

But this verse was clearly for the Jewish people, the sons of Zion.

Then I remembered that if we are born again believers in Christ, we are not only earthen pots created by the Master Potter, we are also grafted into God's family as precious sons and daughters. Which makes us worth our weight in fine gold. Which means, we are really something special. That would be the message I would be taking to these children I was soon to teach: We might not be a perfect vessel, we might even have been broken at some point in life, but we can be redeemed, remade, and still be used because we are really something special and worth our weight in gold in God's eyes.

Years after the Bible class, I was reminiscing about this experience and wondering about why I had been so attached to the wonky looking broken vase I could not throw out, to then later use the vase as a tool to teach a God story. And another Bible story popped into my mind. In the story from John 1, about Jesus healing the blind man, *his disciples asked him, saying, Master, who did sin, this man, or his parents, that he was born blind? Jesus answered, Neither hath this man sinned, nor his parents:*

but that the works of God should be made manifest in him. For all of those years, throughout childhood and on into adulthood, that poor man could not see—all because God had planned that at a future time and place, years down the road, Jesus would heal this man so a miracle could be performed. The blind man, thought by so many to have been born imperfect, had been specifically made that way because he was being held in reserve to one day be available to be used by Jesus to reveal His Father's glory via a miracle.

It made me wonder, could it be possible that God's hands were on my hands that day in pottery class so that I would make an imperfect, broken vase because down *my* road, He already had a children's class lined up for me to teach about how God could use them even if they had flaws and had been broken in some form or fashion?

The only conclusion was that I wouldn't know the answer to that question until I got to heaven.

For now, I often remind myself of what Job said in 33:6: *I am according to thy wish in God's stead: I also am formed out of the clay.* And I, too, can become a usable earthen pot because if God can make me, He can also redeem me and remake me.

That is God's story, and this ol' lump of clay that started off as a "pinch" is trying to stay perfectly centered while sticking to my Father's business.

∽ 27 ∾

Breaking Points

During elementary school years, I sat at Daddy's feet and listened to World War II stories. I've mentioned in other stories published elsewhere that he'd fought as a paratrooper—also trained to use different weapons—in the European theatre and fought in every major battle but one, along with many minor skirmishes. His fragmented stories came in bits and pieces while watching the TV series *Combat* starring Vic Morrow as Sgt. Saunders.

Later, when the movie *A Bridge Too Far* was splashed onto the big screen, Daddy remarked, "That's not the way it happened. It happened like this…by the time we hit the water with our canvas boats, most of the smoke screen had blown away. We were sitting ducks for the machine guns on the opposite side of the river mowing us down. Not until after the river crossing did we realize machine gun nests were hidden behind us, where we'd entered the river.

"There weren't enough paddles for about 15 men to a boat—and when paddles were shot to pieces, rifle butts and helmets were used. When one soldier in front of me slumped over, I grabbed his paddle because bullets had splintered the paddle I'd held. I and one other soldier in our boat made it to the other side of the river that day. And the only reason we survived was because we did a flip off the back of the boat, held onto the boat's rim as we tried kicking against the water to make it to the shore, all the while drifting downriver with bullets whizzing through the water between our legs to land somewhere behind us."

I thought about Daddy's story on that river. He couldn't swim. The experience must have been horrendous for him—die in the boat by bullets or drown in the water by flipping overboard and possibly losing his grip on the boat?

When I was an adult, Daddy opened up more about what he'd lived through. The stories came out in bigger pieces. "When we left New York's harbor, it was under cover of darkness so no one would know we'd shipped out. They didn't want the news leaked to Germans. The sea was so rough on the way to northern Africa, that when the ship climbed a mountain of water, my knees met my chin. On the downhill slide into a deep valley-like trough on the backside of darkness, I held onto railings or anything tied down, to keep my balance and not tumble forward. Meal times were the worst—fish with heads intact. I couldn't stand looking at those eyeballs even though I'd fished my entire life. For weeks I survived on chocolate bars until I saw Africa."

That's the way Daddy's stories poured out. Yet something was missing: Emotion. Smells. Fears. Daddy had been telling stories like someone reading facts from history books. Occasionally, he'd go off on a tangent and tell the tale creatively, but most of the stories were simply factual. It was my job as a writer working to compile a few of these stories for future generations to make sure I had details correct while capturing the emotions, sights, and smells on paper. Also, Mother told me that Daddy had had nightmares for years after he'd returned home. What were those nightmares about? I needed details. What was Daddy reliving when his eyelids closed and his mind was supposedly resting?

"Fear was definitely present," Daddy said. "Some men had strong feelings they wouldn't make it through a battle and gave away belongings before the big event. One guy lit a cigarette before the river crossing and then threw the fancy lighter his wife had sent him for Christmas into the bushes saying, 'Guess I won't be needing that anymore.' He didn't live to tell about the crossing."

"Daddy, did you ever have that feeling that you weren't going to make it out alive before going into a battle?"

"No. Never did. There were plenty though, who did. One guy, right before a battle in Italy—he was going to shoot his big toe off so he could miss the fight. He didn't realize that the shot fired would take off half his foot. Poor guy. I had volunteered to fight and occasionally volunteered for special missions on top of my regular duties when they needed something extra, like taking a string of mules with supplies to our soldiers on top of a mountain in Venafro, Italy. As a farm boy, I knew how to handle mules. Fighting was my job. Most of us got down to it. When it was my turn to fight atop that mountain—mountains that were as steep as the North Carolina Appalachian Mountains—there was one soldier who had been hit real bad. We faced machine gun fire, mortars, and strafing airplanes. There wasn't one inch of that boy's jumpsuit fabric that wasn't drenched in red blood. They tied him to a rock to keep him from rolling off the mountain. He moaned and cried out all night. Equipped with a shot of morphine, as were all paratroopers who jumped behind enemy lines, I let somebody else shoot him up to ease his pain. Giving shots was one thing I had no stomach for."

We then began to talk about Dan Hueval Woods. The Devils Den as the Americans called it. A place right in the middle of an apple orchard. "Right after *The Bridge Too Far* incident, Company I—or the handful of us that was left of it—was ordered into The Devil's Den to keep the German soldiers out. They'd been going in first thing in the morning and firing on the Allied soldiers."

"Maybe they were going in for the apples too," I suggested. "If you and your comrades were starving, you know they were probably hungry as well."

"Maybe, but mostly they wanted to hang onto previously claimed ground and take out our soldiers," Daddy said. "When dusky dark rolled around, the Germans left their fox holes for safer ground. And that's when the paratroopers silently moved in and took up residence in their holes. But not without a fight. The Germans somehow knew we were there and tried sneaking back in to slit throats. No way did I sleep that night. No way was I getting my throat slit. Come first light of day, the battle for possession began. Incoming was so hot apples exploded everywhere.

"I saw Captain Kitchen make a break and run. I thought if my commander was giving up the fight it was time to haul out of there before German tanks blew me out of my foxhole, which had just happened to men in front of me. The last I saw of the captain, soldiers were helping him under the barbed wire fence, dragging him to safety. Looked like he'd been wounded.

"The guy next to me said, 'Let's get outta here!' I stayed long enough to sling the sights from my bazooka as far as I could so the Germans couldn't use it on me later, and followed my foxhole buddy to safety. Tracers whizzed all around, kicking dirt up around my feet and zipping past my head. When I ripped through the barbed wire, I sprinted for my life. At one point, I was winded so bad, I had to rest behind a skinny tree that in no way protected me. Looking to my right, there were two Germans ducking behind their tank to keep out of the line of fire. They looked at me, I looked at them, and none of us fired. I had no energy, could hardly catch my breath, and the enemy was simply trying to stay alive. When I got my breath back, I ran as fast as I could back to my lines and promptly asked about the commander. 'Was he shot?'

"'No,' said a soldier. 'His stomach…his nerves were so bad he doubled over and had to be dragged to safety.'

"The captain was a brave soldier. He wouldn't have caved in when it came to a fight. It was then I knew every soldier had a breaking point."

At one point in my questioning, Daddy broke down, softly sobbing. I'd never seen him cry about war exploits. He was the toughest of the tough even though he wasn't a big man. (At the beginning of the war, the military used shorter men because they made a smaller target. During the war, attrition was so bad they later took anyone they could get.) Before Daddy transferred from regular army—right after Pearl Harbor, his commanding officer (CO) told him he shouldn't transfer.

"Don't do it," his CO said. "Those paratroopers are crazy." Daddy replied, "If I'm going to war, I want the toughest of the tough to have my back."

And while Daddy had talked about his war stories for years to his children without showing any emotion, it was only when I was an adult and pressed for details and asked for specifics that he broke. I was shocked and saddened that such horrible experiences could bring tears after so many years. I'd thought time healed….

That's when I recalled a childhood incident. Mother had walked out onto our icy front porch to get a previously delivered glass milk jug. When she slipped and fell, the gallon jug broke, cutting her wrist. Blood flowed like small rivulets among embedded shards of glass.

Daddy walked from the kitchen where he'd been drinking coffee and smoking cigarettes—his daily morning ritual before breakfast—to see what had happened. When he saw the blood, he said, "That looks bad." Frozen into place, Daddy showed no emotion. No tender caring. No, "Let me see that" or "Honey, I'm so sorry, how can I help?" I can't recall many details, but he might have even been aggravated. He always seemed to get angry when I got hurt. At least he did ask Mother, "Do you need for me to take you to the emergency room?"

Mother, through her tears and pain, shot back, "I'll drive myself." I watched from the bathroom door as she sat on the commode and pressed a washcloth to her hand and wrist and cried. *Why wouldn't my daddy—the toughest man in the world who'd survived jumping behind enemy lines on numerous occasions killing the enemy who threatened to kill him and his family and country's way of life—insist on driving my mother to the hospital?* I watched in anguish as mother dressed and drove from the house with a blood soaked towel around her wounds. I hurt for days over this incident. *Why hadn't Mother insisted he drive her? What was happening that I was missing?*

It wouldn't be until I was writing a story for *Broken Moments* 55 years later that I would understand this scenario. Daddy's breaking point was seeing blood. He couldn't stand to see the sight of human blood and that's why I hid my cut toe in the dirt one time when I was 10 years old. Daddy could no longer cope with seeing someone hurt. He'd seen enough blood and mangled flesh to last a couple of lifetimes.

He'd been wounded in Naples, Italy by friendly fire and had shrapnel dug out of the back of his leg—for which he'd received a Purple Heart.

"It was nothing," Daddy said. "Guys were asking for Purple Hearts for cutting their fingers on K-Ration cans. I was no hero. Purple Hearts meant nothing to me. I went right back into the fight after being wounded. They needed every man on the front lines. I only did my job."

All of the blood he'd seen during the war—the traumatic experiences—had to be why he was always agitated when I cut myself or scraped a knee or Mother injured herself. That was why he ate more Tums and Alka-Seltzer, smoked more cigarettes, and drank more coffee than anybody I ever knew, especially during episodes when his family was hurt or bleeding.

No wonder he'd never mentioned the blood shed by Jesus in our private talks about the Bible. The "mystery" mentioned in the New Testament, yes. And "Where do you think Paradise is?" yes. Never *The Blood*.

Thank God He sent His Son, Jesus, to shed blood for all, especially Daddy, so he wouldn't have to suffer and shed copious amounts himself. My father had seen enough blood to last a lifetime. At last, incidents that had happened in my past made sense. Finally, I had a better understanding of breaking points.

◈ 28 ◈
Swimming to Cuba

I'd finally gotten over my fear of deep water—okay, maybe not totally and that could possibly be classified as a white lie or a fib—and decided to take scuba diving lessons because a young family teen I knew and will call Jacob (not his real name) really wanted to scuba dive. If I didn't learn to scuba dive and get over my fear of deep water, Jacob couldn't take scuba diving lessons since I was the only one who could break away that summer to travel with him for certification in Florida.

My fancy new gear smelled similar to the interior of a new car. Or maybe that was my imagination. Whatever, I was pumped, looking like a banana with dark blue stripes down my diving "skin." Mask and fins matched—bright yellow—and I was equipped with an underwater flashlight and a knife. I was Lloyd Bridges Juniorette.

I practiced in the shallow end of the indoor pool. But something didn't seem quite right about my new mask. My dive instructor, Bud, told me to spit in the mask, swirl the spit around to keep the mask from fogging, and all would be okay. Spit duties taken care of, the night for the deep-water diving test had come. I had to pass this last step to get certified for the final test. In the deep end of the indoor swimming pool, the mask not only fogged, water trickled in, finding its way up my nose. I felt like the *Titanic* going down never to resurface. fought my way to the surface in full panic mode; a barracuda zooming for something shiny, like the metal ladder and the sign above the door that said "EXIT."

I tried to lug myself from the pool, calling it quits, but the instructor grabbed me from the middle of a step and pulled me back into the deep, me trying to free myself so I could escape. He then twirled me around in the water, held onto my vest at the shoulders, and began talking right in my face, eyeball to eyeball, nostril to nostril, eyebrow to eyebrow, trying to calm me down like an exorcist right before demanding demons to leave in the name of Jesus.

"Come on, now. Calm down. It's okay. It's the mask, we'll get you one that fits. This occasionally happens. Don't worry, stay calm, piece of cake, this mask just doesn't fit you right. Once you get properly fitted, you can do this. Breathe deep. Breathe. That's it. Breathe. Now get back in there and swim!"

I semi-believed Bud, felt some of my demons leaving to look for another "house," and then saw Jacob's woe-is-me eyes and sad sack face. Feeling sorry for Jacob because I was killing his up 'til now, lifetime dream, I tried to act like a mature adult and get my act together. I agreed to go to the dive shop and look for a different mask the next day, but later—after I suffered through all the bravery and bravado I could muster up, I tried to find a brown bag in case I hyperventilated in heavy traffic on the way home.

Turned out Bud was right. The mask didn't fit properly and a diver doesn't really know for sure a mask fits perfectly until the trial run. By the skin of my eye tooth, and possibly lunch residue caught in a back molar—broccoli—I passed all I needed to pass. I finished second-to-last swimming all of the laps. There was only one slower, out of a class of about eight. I didn't feel so bad because the one slower was a guy. If I'd had spinach for lunch instead of broccoli, perhaps I could have been third to last. Of course, Jacob was in the top echelon of the class. He could swim like a shark sniffing Top Predator bloody-chum.

Then it was Road Trip! to Islamorada in the Florida Keys. Once there, I was paired with Jacob who seemed to be having adrenaline issues. After we got off the boat and into the water, he, too, was journey proud and wanted to swim to Cuba, unlike me, a diver totally comfortable with swimming in circles around the anchor line like we'd been instructed to do. The problem was, Bud had told us the water was murky with bad visibility and to stay close to the anchor line, but Jacob was having none of that.

I tried to be a good buddy on the buddy system, however, the normally sweet and docile teen was acting like he'd just been freed from the house after a month's grounding from the keys to Dad's car. I had a difficult time keeping up with him. Finally, I reached him and signaled we needed to turn around and go back.

Jacob shook his head and pointed toward Cuba. I underwater-argued, shook my head and made loud noises with my vocal chords that came out garbled to my ears, then pointed back to the boat. Jacob would not comply. I made a slashing sign across my neck and violently pointed toward the surface. Once up top, I looked behind me. I spotted the boat a half-mile away, maybe not that far—but I didn't plan on measuring distance. If there was a shark nearby, we were shark chum. Dead meat. If one of us had a problem, there was no one near enough to hear a call for help. "Listen," I said, "We're going back."

"No," Jacob said, trying to wheedle me into moving forward and beyond the horizon. He was all about putting as much distance as possible between us and the boat. There was this new "air" gathered about him. If I was the Lloyd Bridges Juniorette, Jacob was Lloyd Bridges Senior on steroids. "Let's keep swimming," said Jacob-Lloyd Sr.

Not liking what was happening one bit, but since Jacob wasn't my biological child, instead of giving him a direct order I said, "We were told before we left the boat to stay close to the anchor line." I then vehemently argued. "We can't see all that much down there anyway. We'll be swimming in circles soon because there's no visibility down there past 15 feet. We can't even see *the boat* from down there. What's the purpose in swimming so far out? We're supposed to be looking at coral and fish."

"No."

God, help me stay calm or I could totally end up like a Titanic victim at the bottom of the sea or in the belly of a huge fish!

I then gave the direct order. "We're going back."

If I'd had the fly swatter I used on my own kids, I would have used it on him then and there.

Jacob-Lloyd shook his head.

"Listen," I said, "I'm deathly ill." White lie. Not deathly ill. Just plain ol' *ill* at this teen's behavior. But then quite suddenly, a sinking feeling crept into the deepest part of my stomach and "deathly ill" seeped in. I became truly nauseated just thinking about the excuses I would give his parents when returning home without him. *Um, I don't know how to tell you this but, Jacob and I ended up in Cuba, were tried as spies, and when I was freed from prison, they didn't free Jacob.* Or, *About five miles out from the boat, your precious son was swallowed by a whale. I expected any minute for the whale to spit him out, but it was getting close to dinner time and I had to head back to the boat. Last I saw, the whale was headed toward Greenland.*

All kinds of craziness was running through my brain.

Really wanting to lose what little breakfast was still left in my stomach now, I said in the most authoritative tone I could muster, "*I'm* going back and *you're* going back with me. You're *my* responsibility. Start *swimming*." Was that ever one hot teen—and by *hot* I do mean *mad*. When we made it back to the boat, the divers were surfacing for lunch. I hated to do it, because I was a daredevil myself and had once been a young and carefree kid who'd experienced some crazy and wild death defying adventures, but I could feel more gray hairs coming in as I contemplated what I was being forced to do. I had no choice. I ratted out Jacob to the Dive Master. Now Bud was bristling hot.

"So you tried to swim to Cuba did you?" Then came the take-down lecture. Bud was not treading lightly. He re-paired us, putting Jacob with an older guy in his late 20s who wouldn't take no for an answer the first time. I felt horrible. Jacob developed a severe headache from embarrassment and asked to stay as my diving buddy. Bud would not relent. Smart guy.

That night, Bud found out that while we'd been diving earlier, there was another dive crew not far from us also on a final certification trip. I'd seen them not too far off; our boat had followed in their wake headed out to sea earlier. Long story short, one of the guys wasn't scuba diving—only snorkeling. But he made a huge diving error. He took a deep breath, made a free dive about thirty feet or more to hook up with a friend who was on the bottom looking at coral, exhaled, then took another breath off of his friend's regulator before heading back to the top. There was one crucial problem with this brilliant scheme to view the bottom of the ocean: He hadn't been trained to slowly exhale as he was ascending, therefore, he experienced pulmonary barotrauma. In layman's terms, his lungs ruptured.

"Did he make it?" one of my crew asked as I felt my face free-falling.

Bud shook his head. "Afraid not. He died." Talk about a Titanic moment! All were horrified. All of us sensed what could have come next, *That's why, when I tell you to dive around the anchor line, it's for your own safety you dive around the anchor line!* But Bud didn't have to say it. I could sense he knew we were all thinking about Jacob. And that not far off that day, someone was killed while on a lark, having fun.

Then I knew. That sick, sinking feeling I'd had earlier—like the *Titanic* going under never to rise again—had been my and Jacob's protection. I'd become stressed to the max for a life or death reason.

Because of that trip and that experience, Jacob learned a huge lesson, even though it was at someone else's life-giving expense. But for that day, Jacob was given life and was thankful to live so he could experience more of life along with more dive trips. Today, he's the proud father of a quiver of children, with tall tales to pass down to those kids—like that time he tried to swim to Cuba.

~ 29 ~
Never So Thrilled to See a Toilet

I thought I'd had it with toilets. I have a love/hate relationship with them. Always looking for one when out in public and always repairing one in private. Most every single one of my "thrones" has eventually leaked or overflowed, or had "the whine," that sound one makes when the bobber thingie in the tank won't float to the top, causing excessive water bills because the water runs nonstop. Throughout the years, I've had so many potties fixed that even though I know toilets are a necessity, to think about them wore me out.

Until something big happened in the ancient world. Here's the story:

I never thought I'd live to see the day that I'd be thrilled to see an old toilet turn up. But when archaeologists discovered a commode during a dig in the ancient town of Lachish, located southwest of Jerusalem, I happy danced through my house. Because this wasn't just any old commode. This was the toilet referred to in 2 Kings 10:27: *They brake down the image of Baal, and brake down the house of Baal, and made it a draught house (latrine) unto this day.* This toilet was placed there by King Jehu for a reason. And the truth was finally made known: He really did destroy idols and turn Lachish into a latrine as the Bible claims.

But let me share the background to this story. After Jehu, commander of fellow officers, was anointed king of Israel by a man from the company of the prophets through instructions given by the prophet Elisha, the same man gave Jehu a message from God as he poured the oil on Jehu's head and declared, *Thus saith the Lord God of Israel, I have anointed thee king over the people of the Lord, even over Israel. And thou shalt smite the house of Ahab thy master, that I may avenge the blood of my servants the prophets, and the blood of all the servants of the Lord, at the hand of Jezebel. For the whole house of Ahab shall perish: and I will cut off from Ahab him that pisseth against the wall, and him that is shut up and left in Israel: And I will make the house of Ahab like the house of Jeroboam the son of Nebat, and like the house of Baasha the son of Ahijah: And the dogs shall eat Jezebel in the portion of Jezreel, and there shall be none to bury her. And he opened the door, and fled.* 2 Kings 9:6-10

From this ancient biblical account, God was serious about His instructions that no one should worship idols and His commandment: "Thou shalt have no other gods before me." So he anointed Jehu, whose name means "God is he," as king to usurp the throne of king Ahab who had—along with his wife Jezebel who practiced sorcery and witchcraft—been worshipping the false god Baal.

After reading about that ancient find, I began to think God had a funny sense of bathroom humor—at least when He was fed up with disobedient humans. Whatever the case, I now love talking about toilets, at least that one found in Israel anyway.

And when I tell people about the commode that's been uncovered from antiquity, I also tell them about another thing

I've discovered from modern times: universal toilet guts do not fit inside every brand. So don't be fooled when it comes to idol worshipping or toilet gut intricacies. They're both something you don't play around with because there are repercussions with either one.

I hope this bit of news has been a blast from the past, and will also give the reader something new to think about when visiting your own home throne. Much better than thinking about that chain you will have to hook up again because for some reason, they always slip through the tiniest gap in the little triangle you have to fish for when the toilet won't flush.

The good news is, when we get to heaven we will be made perfect. I hope that means we'll also no longer need a commode. The only thrones we'll see will be the ones where God is seated along with His One and Only at His right hand. Thank you Jesus!

~ 30 ~
The Rack of Ribs That Got Away

The world today is a busy one. People run here and there trying to complete a work day. Later, they're swamped and hurried trying to get their children to athletic events and church, if they can even squeeze God in—and there's no time to sit on the front porch to swing a while.

So imagine my surprise when I heard my doorbell ring. Who could it be? Unless family stood at the door, no way was I getting out of my pajamas to speak with anyone. I had work to do on my computer. Nope. Not going to hustle to get changed to answer the door.

But allow me to flashback to a year before.

I'd gone out to get the mail one night and the new neighbor had waved at me from the shadows the street lamp made on her driveway. I waved back at her before stepping back inside.

A week later I drove to a barbeque joint to purchase take out: a pork sandwich with slaw and fries. To use an old expression my grandmother once used—my eyes were bigger than my stomach, and I also bought a rack of beef ribs. Way too much for me to eat. But when hunger pains start, I want everything on the menu and tend to "over" order.

Once I'd scarfed down the sandwich and fries, no way could I eat an entire rack of ribs. I couldn't eat one rib. What had I been thinking? Hmmm. I could put them in the fridge and eat some tomorrow. But instead, there was a nudge to give them away.

Lord, are you kidding? Ribs are expensive!

Immediately, I no longer had a desire for ribs and knew where they were supposed to go. The new neighbors who'd just moved in down the street.

"Seriously Lord? It's pitch black outside and totally inappropriate for me to go ringing doorbells after dark.

"Okay then. I'll do it.

"Hopefully, they will accept the ribs and appreciate not having to cook as much supper after trying to unpack and set up house all week. I am going to feel like a fool though, ringing somebody's doorbell this late.

"I'm always feeling like Jeremiah the weeping prophet. You had him do some crazy stuff too."

There wasn't yet a shade or curtain over the neighbor's front door. I could see clear through the hallway to the kitchen and gathered it was the husband-dad headed for the door.

God, I look like a peeping Tom. I hope he doesn't think I'm an aggravating neighbor coming over here to be nosy or worse, a serial killer.

"Hi," I said, embarrassed to be ringing his doorbell since I loved my peace and quiet and didn't relish someone ringing *my* doorbell and interrupting me when I was busy. "I really hate to bother you, um, I'm your neighbor two houses down. I honestly have no idea why I bought this much food tonight, there's no way I can eat all of this. It was one of those 'my eyes were bigger than my stomach' moments, but if you'd like to have this pan of extra ribs, you're welcome to them. Again, no way I can eat all of this."

I witnessed that man's eyes lighting up like full moons. He had to be a Southerner because only a few things can make a Southern man's eyes light up like that: Hunting season, fishing season, football season, and barbeque anything season.

He didn't hesitate to extend his arms to reach toward me to relieve me of my pan. "My wife's not home yet, so I'd be more than happy to get those ribs!"

He didn't even say, "Aw shucks, that's awfully nice of you but why don't you just freeze 'em for tomorrow?"

Trust me, I'd been working on a reply, "Well, in that case, why don't I just split 'em with you?"

But he was not giving one of those ribs back.

So, I handed over the meat and introduced myself properly. Kind of. "Just thought I'd also welcome you to the neighborhood while I'm here. I promise you'll rarely see me, I have plenty to keep me busy. Hope you enjoy the ribs."

Translation: *I stay clear of HOA meetings.*

I thought "that was the end of that." I'd done my neighborly duty and I hoped against all hope their dog wouldn't bark at me every time he saw me in my back yard digging, planting, mulching, and weeding. (I soon learned their pup would bark at me every time he caught me outside.)

Imagine my surprise, when now, several months later, my doorbell rang, and through the camera I saw that same neighbor with his little family.

Nope, you caught me in my cat jammies eating peanut butter Reese's cups and I'm not opening the door. I don't have any more ribs.

After a few minutes of staring at my shrubbery, I heard the dad say, "Just leave it on the mat."

What were they leaving on the mat? Hmmmm. I waited until I thought they'd gone home and slowly opened the door. There in front of me was a gorgeous bouquet of flowers. That little boy had seen a neighbor bring his family food one night and here was his chance to return the favor with a random act of kindness.

When I think back on the exchanges, I know there was a higher power in the mix. It's a truly rare thing for me to buy an entire rack of ribs. God knew where those ribs were going before they were even passed to me to ride shotgun back home.

And the bouquet of flowers? There were two ranunculus flowers in the mix. I'd had ranunculus flowers on my mind for weeks but it was still too cold to try and get the octopus looking bulbs started in my garage. God not only knew there was a hungry man down the street when I walked down the sidewalk and handed over those ribs, God also knew my woman's heart. I'd been gifted back via a flower bouquet, and in that bouquet were the ranunculus flowers I'd longed for. The first time anyone had ever given me that particular flower. Peonies, I could grow. The knack for growing ranunculus flowers evaded me.

After my surprise, I noticed another surprise. On one of my front shrubs was a strand of lights left over from Christmas a month before.

When I'd gathered up all of the other lights, how did I miss that set? How embarrassing!

I had to laugh.

So now, my new neighbor was probably thinking, "That woman must be off her rocker. She left one bush still decorated for Christmas. Now I know why she brought me those ribs because nobody in their right mind would give an entire rack of ribs away!"

And, this, dear Lord, is why I'd rather not welcome new neighbors. They might pay me back with a random act of kindness and laugh about one lone strand of Christmas lights I missed still on one bush well after the season! At least I made the new neighbors laugh.

Delight thyself also in the Lord: and He shall give thee the desires of thine heart. Psalm 37:4

~ 31 ~
From One Who Loves Her Country

Coming from a family who's had a long line of men involved in fighting our country's wars as far back as the Revolutionary War, I have been a patriot since I was a child sitting at the feet of my father who was a paratrooper in WWII, as I've previously mentioned. His first jump behind enemy lines was in Sicily where he and two comrades were lost for three days with one egg to be boiled and divided between them, along with a hunk of bread that was so hard, "You could knock a mule down with it and we had to boil it, then dip it into our hot coffee to eat it."

And as previously mentioned in my writings, I watched *Combat!*—a 60s TV series starring Vic Morrow and Rick Jason—during the week with Daddy and scenes in the television show revived other war stories he shared with me. Allow me, readers, to refresh your memory about the time he was awarded a Purple Heart—the time he was wounded in Naples, Italy. "I was hit by friendly fire, shrapnel in the back of the thigh. The doc said, 'I don't have anything for pain. Bend over and hang onto that barrel' and proceeded to dig the metal out with tweezers. They only had two Purple Hearts at

Command Post and there had been three of us wounded in the barrage so I let the other two soldiers get theirs. Medals didn't mean that much to me. Guys were cutting their fingers while opening their bean cans and yelling, 'I'm wounded! I get a Purple Heart!'" What did mean something to Daddy was staying alive to finish the war Hitler started so he could make it back home. (He received his Purple Heart later.)

There was one point, after a big battle, Daddy and a couple of others performed a grisly task. "Six of us took the body of my assistant gunner down the hill to the valley. Two troopers stood guard on the flanks while four of us carried his corpse. We loaded our burden onto the jeep and watched it drive the deceased soldier away. Returning to our positions, we came upon abandoned foxholes where hard tack crackers and discarded containers had been left. We ransacked the tins and gorged ourselves. We hadn't had any K-rations brought up to the front lines and food was scarce. We were ravenous. At times we scavenged the dead for ammunition and food. Peaches. Candy bars. Beans. Cigarettes. Whatever the dead men had left in the pockets of their jump suits that we could eat or use to kill. During this particular time of scavenging, I looked up and saw our distinguished regimental commander, Colonel Tucker, watching us from a bombed out house with no glass in the windows."

"Daddy," I said, "were you ever embarrassed for your commander to see you robbing the dead?"

"You can't embarrass a starving man. And he knew his men were hungry and low on ammunition. When the war was over, I swore I'd never go hungry again.

"During the battle now known as 'A Bridge Too Far' during Operation Market Garden, a British General said the daylight river crossing of the Waal River to save the Nijmegen Bridge was a suicide mission. 'They'll never make it. They'll turn back.' Colonel Tucker watched as his men were slaughtered and said, 'They may not make it, but you won't see the first boat turn back.' Colonel Tucker was right. Not one of us turned back. We lost 60 percent of our men in the first wave. The man in front of me in our canvas boat got hit. I grabbed his paddle because mine had been shattered from my hands by bullets. We paddled with helmets and hands.

"One day we got word that the Germans had lined up around 17 American soldiers and mowed them down instead of taking them prisoners. After hearing that, my men and I made a pact: 'We will never surrender. We will fight to the death.'

"And fight until death we did. Out of a company of 125 soldiers, approximately five men who fought with me through the entire war made it home alive. There were some who left the company through attrition if they broke a leg, foot, or ankle. After that, they couldn't be trusted to not favor that leg and might break their good leg. So those guys were profiled down and ended up in another outfit. The generals needed every warm body to fight.

"One of the scariest moments was when we were loaded onto LCI's (landing boats). We saw Stuka dive-bombers headed toward us. They bombed some of our boats. I saw the first bomb leave a plane. Squeezed in shoulder to shoulder, we hit the deck. Our boat—filled with soldiers from Company I—rolled over, listing at a 90° angle. I thought the boat would flip and crush us. I couldn't swim. Company G's boat was next to us, broken nearly in half; I saw daylight through it before it sank. It didn't have far to sink since we were close to shore and stuck on a sand bar. We took our life preservers and inflated them and threw them into the sea for the wounded. Most had missing body parts.

"Our catwalk was lowered and we were ordered into the water. I wondered how long it would take the sharks to smell our blood. Sinking into deeper water without my life jacket, I ditched my bazooka, rifle, grenades and ammunition, until my bedroll popped me back to the top. I dog paddled to beat 90 before my bedroll became water logged and dragged me to the bottom of the ocean. The shoreline seemed miles away. Staggering out of the water with pistol in hand, the only weapon I managed to save, I crawled and clawed through the sand until I could get off the beach and find cover. I picked up a dead soldier's rifle until I could rendezvous with the commanding officer, who handed out more weapons. After battles, we gambled at cards and drank Italian vino from castles—distractions until the next battle."

Daddy's stories were endless since he fought through every major battle but one, many smaller skirmishes behind enemy lines, and also while on the front lines facing the German's weapons. He slept in muddy foxholes, some filled with rainwater or snow. He struggled on maneuvers to bodily plow through five feet of snow though frostbitten feet plagued him. There were times he washed his socks with diesel fuel from tanks, not having a fresh pair for 75 days. And during those freezing days, he and his men were ordered to shave daily so if they were killed or captured the Germans would think they were fresh troops.

One day, during a time of Daddy reliving all of his escapades, I asked, "Did you ever pray during the war?"

"No. My buddy John and I noticed the chaplain holding a Sunday morning service atop a steep mountain in Venafro, Italy. When the German airplanes began strafing us, the God-fearing men jumped into their foxholes faster than John and I did and we laughed about it later: 'They don't have any more faith than we do!' But Mama and Aunt Willie's entire church prayed for me back home while I was fighting."

"God knew you weren't saved and perhaps that's why He let you live."

"Maybe so. It would take me having to fly back from the war over an ocean for me to turn to the Lord. I was afraid of being shot down by submarines whose captains hadn't heard the war was over—and we were flying low above the white caps of the sea to avoid radar and subs. I was petrified because I still couldn't swim. I promised God I'd quit gambling and drinking if He'd spare me and get me home. He took me at my word. Once home, I was baptized in the Tennessee River."

Years later, every July Fourth my family and extended family gathered at my parents' farm to celebrate our country's freedom won by the sacrifices our ancestors made. The picnic tables groaned under so much food. Lots of barbeque, watermelons, and veggies too numerous to count. In the cool of the garage four ice cream freezers hummed to the tune of four different flavors—peach, chocolate, vanilla, and strawberry. Cakes and pies galore beckoned from tables beneath the pines. Daddy sent fresh vegetables from his garden home with the little old great aunts who gathered with us. He always planted more than he and Mother could eat so he could help others. He held to his promise that he would never go hungry again and when he slaughtered a heifer from his cattle herd, my freezer was also loaded. When Mother canned vegetables, my pantry was delighted. The good Lord blessed the work of my parents' hands. I was fortunate to have been reared in the city on week days, raised on a farm on weekends and summers. Lucky to have a God-fearing family.

Fast forward to present times and our country getting involved in wars we have no business being in. As an adult, learning that there is a boatload of money to be made by the military industrial complex President Eisenhower warned us about before he left office, and about big corporations who manufacture weapons and whose best interest is to keep the flow of money moving in their direction, was eye opening.

I think about how my grandparents and others lived with rationing during WWII. It was almost impossible to get sugar; tires were needed for jeeps and other military vehicles; silk was used for parachutes instead of silk stockings, and the protein from meat was needed for our fighting men—all for the war effort to keep our country free. Yet, we have people to this day in higher offices in Washington D.C. who never helped fight a war in their lifetime and who scheme to get wealthy off of insider trading, kickbacks, and various under-the-table deals with communist countries who plot and plan to control our rich and benevolent country. Though there are those in power who allowed God-fearing teachers to be removed from our schools and universities while also keeping God's name totally out of our schools, America is still an incredible country to live in. However, our country is changing every day and in some scenarios, in frightening ways.

Even though the devil has a toehold into our country via communism and Marxism infiltrating every government office, people from all over the world still want to come to this country so their families can prosper so they, too, can live the American dream or die trying.

For now, we are free because our ancestors fought and died for that freedom. In Philadelphia, 1787, as the delegates to the Constitutional Convention were leaving Independence Hall, having decided on the general structure for the new United States, a crowd gathered there to hear the news. It has been said that when a little old lady asked Ben Franklin, "Well, doctor, what do we have, a republic or a monarchy?" Franklin replied, "A republic, if you can keep it." With that reply, Franklin gave us hope and a warning. It will be up to the people to keep the Republic.

And keep it we must, since there are no new continents available. Many countries will not tolerate religious freedom or freedom of speech and have already been overthrown. Our world is on fire in more ways than one.

Therefore, it is up to all of us to do our duty to research candidates for office and vote the most capable man or woman—an honest man or woman who loves God and the United States of America—into office, preferably someone who neither wants to prosper off the backs of others nor has a desire to change our constitution as it was laid out by our founding fathers.

And to our founding fathers and those who followed in

their footsteps who fought and died to keep this country free, I hope I might one day be able to say, "Your sacrifice was not in vain."

As long as I have breath in me, I will continue to pray for America. For we are all warriors when we pray, putting on the armor of God taking advantage of God's supernatural power to thwart our enemies.

Praying, my father discovered after the war, is a Christian's best ammunition.

Finally, my brethren, be strong in the Lord, and in the power of his might. Put on the whole armour of God, that ye may be able to stand against the wiles of the devil. For we wrestle not against flesh and blood, but against principalities, against powers, against the rulers of the darkness of this world, against spiritual wickedness in high places. Wherefore take unto you the whole armour of God, that ye may be able to withstand in the evil day, and having done all, to stand. Stand therefore, having your loins girt about with truth, and having on the breastplate of righteousness; and your feet shod with the preparation of the gospel of peace; Above all, taking the shield of faith, wherewith ye shall be able to quench all the fiery darts of the wicked. And take the helmet of salvation, and the sword of the Spirit, which is the word of God: Praying always with all prayer and supplication in the Spirit, and watching thereunto with all perseverance and supplication for all saints. Ephesians 6:10-18

≈ 32 ≈
Spelunking My Way to Jesus

When I was a teen, I was invited to go "caving" with a professional spelunking group. I couldn't wait to see what was beneath the rocks under my feet. On a steamy hot summer day, wearing hard hats with lights attached, our group approached a small hole in the side of a mountain near Trenton, Georgia.

My first thought was, *What if we meet a bear or happen to wander in on a den of rattlesnakes?*

I was assured the cave we were entering had been searched many times before and "the opening to get into the cave is too small for a bear to squeeze through." Everyone was doubtful we'd encounter any snakes. "Snakes are more fond of underground burrows, stumps, and living beneath rocks above ground."

But what if we crawl into the path of a "lost" snake? At least the person in front of me will meet the snake before I do, I reasoned.

In one section I crawled on my stomach, inching my way forward, and I felt the ceiling of the passage against my back. I detested this part and wanted to yell up ahead,

"Hurry! Get moving!" Spelunking was the first time I realized that I was claustrophobic, but it was too late to turn back as there were spelunkers behind me. I had no choice but to keep crawling forward.

Trying to control my breathing, I had to be patient because some of the guys had broad shoulders and their struggle sessions were real as they tried to make themselves small enough to squeeze through what felt like a tube of toothpaste. There was hardly any wiggle room. Dragging a body with forearms only, when sandwiched in, was challenging.

Geez Louise! I should have asked more questions before accepting this invitation.

At last, the air ahead of us cooled and the lot of us reached a cavernous opening. This was an underground room with large boulders we used as chairs when taking a break while counting heads. At one point, to get to the best part of the cave where we would see stalactites and stalagmites, we had to traverse a place that required us to link arms with the spelunkers on each side of our body—like getting ready to swing our partners do-se-do square dance style but without music.

While attempting to ease our bodies into a deep crevice that V'd down into untold darkness the light from our hard hats couldn't penetrate, I was instructed to place my back and shoulders against the huge rock behind me with my feet planted on the monstrous rock in front of me. Then I had to inch my way to the left along with everyone else. If I slipped, the spelunkers locked via elbows next to me could hold me in place until my dangling feet made purchase again with the other side of the crevice.

"How deep is this crevice?" I asked.

"No one knows."

What? What cave monster is down there in the dark that might reach up and yank me down?

Taller people were luckier than shorter folk. Their backsides didn't have to be as deep into the crevice since their long legs could stay closer to the opening of the wider split at the top of the rocks. I had high hopes my new-found friends would keep me safe in the elbow lock in case my feet couldn't reach the other side of the crevice. At one point, I could barely keep the tip-toe soles of my boots in contact with the facing rock wall. Luckily, the "V" tapered back into solid rock so I could once again walk upright on solid ground.

My thoughts kept going back to the entrance of the cave. I feared I couldn't crawl through that passage again. *What if I get so claustrophobic I pass out? Someone will have to put a rope around me and pull my body out…shivers!*

"Is there an easier way out of here?" I asked.

"Nope," said a spelunker next to me. "Same way we crawled in."

Up ahead I heard water splashing before I smelled it. Fresh underground spring water smells like no other. Clean. Pure. When we reached the waterfall and a large pool of water at the base—what an incredible sight! The stalactites and stalagmites were impressive, however, the pool of water was inviting. Taking the time to splash around cooling down arms, faces, and feet, we then scarfed down sandwiches. Bologna never tasted so good.

When the time came to work our way back outside, I

hoped I could stay calm enough to squeeze back through the tunnel entrance. *I can do this. Breathe. One inch at a time. Just breathe!*

Outside, I was never so thankful to see daylight.

Later, I came across Romans 12:12: *Rejoicing in hope, patient in tribulation, continuing instant in prayer....* And I thought about my spelunking opportunity when I gazed on sights most people never see in a lifetime unless they visit a place like Ruby Falls inside Lookout Mountain, Georgia where an elevator takes tourists down into the bowels of the earth. I reminisced about how, as a teen, I was hopeful that the professional spelunkers would take care of me since I was a novice. I was hopeful about making it through tight squeezes and across deep crevices—my tribulation—I had to inch through until I made it to the good part, the joyful part, of the trip: the waterfall and underground swimming pool.

Looking back on this adventure, I realize I was never faithful in prayer asking the good Lord to help me through the dangerous parts. I was simply devil-may-care—as most teens are—and hopeful I would make it to the other side with the help of my friends.

When I ran across that same Bible verse again years later, I thought once again of my teenage caving caper. And it hit me hard that the entire time I was spelunking, I should have not only been hopeful, I should have been praying to Jesus that He would take care of me and keep the snakes and bears away while He and my guardian angel protected me—for humans aren't always reliable and trustworthy.

Not until I was a more mature Christian did I understand

that only through Jesus do I have any hope at all. Jesus is the only one I can trust to take me from dark to light and hope everlasting.

There is a meme popular on Instagram that says something like this: "Do you need Jesus to go to heaven?" and it gives the reply, "You need Jesus to go to Walmart!"

Which is more eye-opening than humorous now I've read a Vanity Fair article about a Texan mother, Margy Palm, who left for K-Mart 40 years ago to Christmas shop and was kidnapped by the serial killer Stephen Peter Morin. Before leaving her home, "She knelt in her closet and told God she would serve Him however He needed her to that day." Because of her faith, hope, and praying over her captor—sharing about Jesus who loved Morin and could save him, no matter his past, this young mother did not become another statistic. Instead, while driving around with someone who had killed 34 young girls and women and seven men in the period from 1969-1981 (Margy didn't know this until later), she laid her hand on Morin's forehead and said a prayer to cast out demons so he could be free. Then she pulled her Bible journal out of the glove compartment and shared the love of Jesus with her kidnapper. Luckily, she also had a tape in the car with the song "Ride Like the Wind" written and sung by Christoper C. Cross on it that kept her captor happy. The same song I and my family listen to as we fly over the border into Mexico.

After Morin was incarcerated, Margy became his friend while he was on death row waiting to meet the Savior Margy had introduced him to. By the power of the Holy Spirit and through her faith and hope, Margy lived to return to her family to serve God for 40 years and still counting. And Morin? I suspect that like the thief on the cross next to Jesus, a repentant Stephen Morin is with Jesus now in Paradise after dying of lethal injection in 1985 after waiving his appeals.

After reading the article about Margy and Morin, I doubt I'll ever go spelunking again, but I will be going to Walmart and the mall. Going forward in today's crazy world, hanging onto my faith and in His grip, I will be ever more hopeful about my safety. Especially since I'll be taking Jesus with me everywhere I venture after I've asked God, "How can I serve you today?"

Note to self: Keep a Bible with marked verses in the car just in case—never know when God might need me to give some hope to someone who's down on their luck, angry, and all out of hope. And also keep a tape of Christopher C. Cross's song "Ride Like the Wind" in the tape player—anything to keep a serial killer happy while you're trying to cast out demons.

The God of hope fill you with all joy and peace in believing, that ye may abound in hope, through the power of the Holy Ghost."
Romans 15:13

33
Come What May

Without going too deep into details of the 2016 election year, let's just leave it at this: I was shocked to think I would live to see the day that college students would need teddy bears, safe spaces, and Play-Doh to help heal their disappointment over their political candidate not winning. Nor did I ever think they would roam the streets bashing out car windows and blocking streets so people couldn't get to the hospitals during emergencies. Weren't they concerned about love *and* hate?

And all this drama after shootings in Chattanooga—my hometown—Orlando, San Bernardino, and other cities where police officers were hunted and gunned down by cold-hearted murderers. Police officers who were husbands. Fathers. And the first line of defense when law and order was needed. We were supposed to be evolving. Moving forward as a society. Instead, the world was upside down with this kind of behavior.

However, 2016 also brought good news as well. My daughter became pregnant with my third grandchild. After two baby girls, she hoped for a boy. In fact, that thought must have been on her mind because even before she became pregnant, she had a dream. She dreamed she was in the hospital and had to be sedated for the delivery and when she woke up, she asked her husband the news. "Boy or girl?"

"We had a boy! And I named him Howie Adventure!"

"What?" screeched my daughter. "Howie? Howieeeee! Adventure?"

"Well, I thought Howie would go along with the other "H" names of our girls. And you said having a boy after two girls would be an adventure…so…."

My daughter yelled, "Hurry! We have to change the name on the birth certificate. We can't name a child *Howie Adventure*!"

At least 2016 was good for some amusement.

But then, right before the election in November, I began having dreams about babies again. And not about boys wearing baby blue. This wasn't unusual for me—dreaming about an event before it happened. Before my daughter flew home from Denver, Colorado to tell me she was pregnant with her first child, my deceased mother visited me in a dream. She and I had gone to a school in Nashville, Tennessee—a school where my daughter had competed in tennis tournaments in years past. Mother and I were at this school to see a child perform on the school's stage. Approximately four years old, this child had long dark hair. She had her back turned to me, so in the dream, I thought I was seeing my own child when she was that age. Then as dreams usually go, it changed for crazy. Mother and I were in a Walgreen's that seemed to be attached to the same school. I remember thinking in the dream, "This is strange. Drugstores in schools these days." Then suddenly, racks of hand-knitted baby clothes, all in a variegated color of maroon, dark green, and gold caught my attention. Winter colors. There were beautiful dresses with ruffles down the front and in all different sizes from newborn to 4T.

On the next rack hung boy clothes. Knitted pants that buttoned onto knitted shirts—all out of the same variegated thread of winter colors. I gravitated back to the girl dresses as I always did when looking at baby clothes because buying for girls was more fun. Mother never said a word. She simply stood nearby as I examined the intricately knitted ruffles on the gorgeous dresses. Then the dream ended. Mother was gone. I'd had only a couple of dreams about her after she'd passed into the arms of Jesus. And in those two dreams, she never spoke. She was simply there. Observing. As though she watched over my family and me from above.

Imagine my surprise when my daughter called to tell me she was flying home from Denver. Over lunch, she burst out with the good news she was pregnant and constantly ill with nausea. I was happy at first, about a new baby, then saddened. Sad because living so far away, I wouldn't be nearby to be with my daughter to help her. The first year of a child's life is one of so many changes and I would be missing out. My next thought was about the dream.

"Now I know what my dream meant," I said. "You're going to have a girl. She'll be born in winter. What's the due date?"

"January. But what makes you think it will be a girl?"

I told her the dream. Winter colors on the ruffled dresses. I turned away from the boy clothes and was more interested in the girl clothes in the dream. "But what I can't figure out is why I dreamed—in the same dream—you were about three or four years old and performing on a stage in Nashville at a school where you used to play in tennis tournaments when you were in high school."

When my daughter's father-in-law told us he'd dreamed the baby was a boy—"I've even seen his face," he said—I thought, *Perhaps I was wrong.* But a couple of months later, when my daughter said she and her husband were transferring back to Nashville, I knew *my* dream would come true. I felt God had allowed Mother to visit me in a dream to comfort me with the news that a new baby girl was to be born.

I also knew Mother had had dreams come true. She dreamed her uncle Jack was killed in action during World War II. Within a few days, the family received the telegram that he'd been killed on the Pacific island of Leyte. Many years later, she lost her car keys, and that night she dreamed where she'd left them: outside on the rock ledge of the house. She must have placed them there after she'd driven home from work and had become distracted when talking outside with Daddy. So in my family, dreams that came true were a normal happening. And I was holding onto my dream, though if a "Howie Adventure" was in the future, that would be fine as well.

Fast forward several months. A granddaughter was born. When she was older, she performed on stage in the same school in Nashville I had dreamed about. And this child had long dark hair, same as in the dream.

I didn't dream about the second grandchild. However, there was a painting of three females on the bathroom wall in my daughter's home. When I was bathing my granddaughter, I happened to look up at the painting and thought, *that looks like a mom, and before her are two girls headed for a swim in the ocean.* Suddenly, an overwhelming feeling about the second grandchild washed over me. I told my daughter, "You're having another girl." I wasn't wrong.

When news of the third pregnancy reached me, I had three dreams over a couple of months. In the first dream, the blanket the child was wrapped in was pink. I also knew she was a girl. In the other two dreams, the baby I held was again swaddled in pink. I then saw myself walking on a boat deck, carrying the child while negotiating a ledge that tapered back into the boat's hull. To get to the front of the boat, I had to leap from this point, a distance that wasn't safe. I looked down at the deep, murky water and knew that if I tried to jump to the front, I could fall into the water and the babe might drown. The moment after I had this thought in the dream, I was somehow miraculously placed in the front of the boat. All was safe. All was secure. The dream ended. But what did this dream mean? Was there to be a baby girl accompanied by danger and she would miraculously be saved? I shuddered at the thought of danger but rested assured about a miraculous safety net of some sort for this child who was soon to enter the world.

A couple of weeks later, during a cupcake gender reveal, this third grandchild was definitely a girl and not "Howie Adventure." I thought back on my dream. The murky water. The fear. The devil can't know our thoughts, but he can plant doubt and throw darts to worry us via our dreams. During this questionable moment in time, I declared, "Get behind me Satan. I am protected by the blood of Jesus." I would trust in the Lord for all things. Even faced with something murky and dark on the horizon, I would hold onto faith that God would see my family and me through that darkness.

This third child was another C-section baby. The third girl in the bathroom painting. The girl in the painting I thought was a mom, seemed now to be the eldest daughter. My daughter's family would be complete with three daughters. However, it seemed like forever before I received word about the delivery—the surgery had been excruciating and there had been a problem. Could this have been the danger I'd perceived in my dream concerning this child? Or, perhaps the danger would manifest in a future event? I wasn't certain.

What I am certain of is this: "God is our refuge and strength, a very present help in trouble." Psalm 46:1

Throughout life, there will always be adventures. Some adventures will be fun, other adventures like shootings and horrific events around the world will be times of struggling through dark, murky water. The Bible calls these dark adventures trials and tribulations. Yet, come what may, my eyes will forever be on the One—the Light—who has the power to protect and save.

It is good for me to draw near to God: I have put my trust in the Lord GOD, that I may declare all thy works.
Psalm 73:28

ॐ 34 ॐ
Little Joker

While in Nashville, Tennessee, I'd said goodnight to my daughter Peyton and tucked my Grandee into bed. A few minutes of posting on social media accounts and I would be snuggled between the sheets. But then, anyone who logs onto the internet knows best laid plans are always sabotaged by cookies. Not the ones you eat but the ones that snoop out your Google search interest and throw out other leads that keep you up 'til dawn. One of my previous search words happened to be "coyotes."

Someone had posted a YouTube video "Black Coyote Kill" that snagged my interest. The last couple of years I'd been plagued with the critters. Like wild turkeys that had been hunted out of the South years back, coyotes were also making a comeback. Everything was fair game for the devils. Turkeys. Deer. Especially fawns. The coyotes had kept my dogs barking and Sweet Pea the cat tormented by not being able to hunt mice after dark thirty.

When I'd first spotted a coyote while atop my tractor and bush hogging my pastures, I'd thought it was the ugliest dog I'd ever seen. It eyeballed me from weed cover 10 yards away, never taking its gaze off me. It gave me the funny feeling I was being closely watched. But then maybe he was someone's pet who was wounded and only needed help—nothing sinister. On the next pass around with the bush hog, the dog was gone.

Never before hearing of coyotes in Tennessee, I forgot about the incident. Until I began hearing what sounded like a pack of dogs howling at the edge of my yard. The more I thought about it, they sounded like—couldn't be—coyotes. In Tennessee?

I Googled "coyotes" and finally wrapped my brain around the fact I had a possible coyote infestation. They appeared to be multiplying in my neck of the woods like deer ticks, and they needed culling. What I read, along with summer night howls, finally convinced me I had problems.

One story I read was about a man out west who was attacked by three of the wild beasts after his car had broken down and he'd walked for help. That story not only shocked—I'd thought coyotes were afraid of humans and steered clear—but was a wakeup call. What if they attacked an innocent child? Working on my property unarmed, I could end up supper for a coyote pack that might have had bad luck hunting and now thought a human looked mighty tasty.

While in the field walking back to the house from the barn one day, I spotted what first appeared to be a small German Shepherd trotting from my back yard to cross the pasture to the woods. Ice water seemed to flow through my veins as I realized I'd spotted my nemesis. Coyote. Fear enveloped me as I thought of Sweet Pea and my dogs, Rascal and Maverick. Running to the house while also charging the coyote, I yelled. The scoundrel was so brazen he never even turned his head to acknowledge I was a blip on his cruel screen.

The pets were safe for now. My gun was loaded. But I wasn't prepared for what happened next. I heard the dogs barking and ran out to see what they'd cornered.

A coyote stood in the backyard baring his teeth throughout a slow retreat, not in the least afraid of dogs or a human. Stunned at the thought he was outnumbered and prepared to fight with me standing there, I took a couple of shots and missed the moving target before he ran.

I was tired of odiferous whiffs of coyote stench. I needed a rifle. With a scope.

One morning not long after, I heard an odd sound in the courtyard outside my bedroom. Jerking the door open, I stared a coyote in the face—for about one flat heart beat. Just as frightened as I was, he leaped twice for the pasture but forgot about the swimming pool he'd skirted upon sneaking in for an attempted Sweet Pea supper.

I couldn't take a chance on shooting a hole through my pool liner if my trembling hands missed so what happened next with a skimmer pole and me in my nightgown wasn't pretty enough for YouTube. The battle lasted for a gruesome 30 minutes and when it was over, I shook for another 30 thinking about snapping teeth, wild amber eyes, and what could have been. Coyote ugly. I felt sick. These were God-created animals trying to survive an encroaching world.

There had to be a more humane and safer way to rid myself of this nuisance. But the ki-yotes, as some called them, had stepped on my last nerve. Ergo, the reason I was interested in the YouTube video "Coyote Kill."

As I watched the replay of the young hunter patiently

waiting to put another notch on his belt, however, I felt there was something strangely familiar about this kid. Especially when he said the coyote had been tricky to kill and added, "He's been a little joker." The hunter couldn't have been out of high school, yet, I felt like I somehow knew him. I checked the name and location on the video—John (not his real name), Georgia. Memories flooded in. During my high school days, I'd once dated a John from Georgia. He'd been the drummer in a band hired to play at a party and had later asked me for a date. Who could turn down a cute band boy who crooned the words from the Spencer Davis Group, "I'm a man, yes I am and I can't help but love you so...."

And "I'm-a-man" could possibly have passed along his genes to YouTube Coyote Boy.

Suddenly, I was taken back in time. Hot rods were here to stay, hot pants were on their way in, and Jerry Reed's song "When You're Hot You're Hot" was climbing its way up the charts. Back in the early 1970s, all of the teenagers old enough to drive in north Georgia ended up across the state line at the Chattanooga, Tennessee, Brainerd Road Shoney's Drive-in after a movie, cruising the lot to see and be seen before sliding into a vacant parking spot to order chow. If you were a guy and anybody—a.k.a. high school cool—you arrived with arm candy.

Not part of the cool crowd, I spent many nights alone either with my Bible open working on a lesson or with a National Geographic Magazine planning on majoring in anthropology along with archaeology while in college. I had serious plans to dig up man's bones. Warming them—not so much. Having attended a sex education class, I was pretty savvy about what happened when a female got close enough to warm a man's bones. I was not a total geek. A family was in my picture, but down the road. College and traveling were first on my agenda. I had some goals to achieve in life before marriage and a baby carriage. Heaven forbid the baby carriage coming first.

One can only imagine my dilemma on the first date with John at Shoney's when he stole a kiss. Right there in front of God and everybody cruising the grounds, I received one of the most passionate kisses I've ever had in my life. Possibly a nine-pointer on the Richter scale. A *have mercy* moment, I thought the entire world was smokin' and I was afraid John's silver Camaro with black racing stripes was going to burst into flames before I could untangle my singed lips. I thanked the Lord when the carhop arrived with a slightly warm cheeseburger to cool things off.

Problem was, I couldn't enjoy the bliss of that kiss. Well, maybe I enjoyed the fiery moment for the length of a frog's hair and kissed him back for a New York minute—*grinning big here*—but mostly, I was too busy worrying about who was going to see me in the arms of I'm-a-man-and-I-can't-help-but-love-you-so. This boy was Trouble with a capitol "T" and I heard warning bells. If he would steal a kiss in public what would he do in private? All I could think about was my parents grounding me for life. I'd never advance my education by screaming, "Go Vols," at the University of Tennessee and studying under the world renowned forensic anthropologist Dr. Bass, much less trekking to some archaeological dig in the steamy jungles of Africa.

And what if the preacher, who sometimes made house calls, got wind of my escapades and paid a visit to tell me kissing could lead to something else, and diapers, and I was kicked out of junior choir and Wednesday night Girl's Auxiliary and would be replaced posthaste as Mother Mary in the upcoming Christmas play? Becoming a fallen angel was not on my senior year bucket list. I'd already invested time in memorizing Mary's lines and had the baby Jesus swaddled.

I don't recall any more face time that fateful night, however, I did agree to another date. A double date. Safety in numbers. We drove to the Chickamauga Battlefield. Right up my historical alley. A big Civil War buff, my thinking was with more people along, no way could I get into a compromising situation while studying Johnny Reb flanking maneuvers.

The problem was, my Johnny Reb's treasure trove of battle plans held more than one maneuver. In fact, John had out-flanking maneuvers he hadn't yet used. After reading a battlefield marker, the guys ran to the hotrod. Hopped in. And eased a couple of feet away. When I tried to open the car door, Johnny Reb again eased the car forward, a tad more, until the door handle was out of my grasp. After a few times of "he's been a little joker," John drove off leaving me standing in the middle of the forest eating dust. Furious, I turned to my female companion. "If this is a joke…it's…not…funny," I said, gritting out each word through clenched teeth. "We should hide and not be here when, and if, they return. Hike out to the ranger's station. And call home for a ride."

The only thing about calling home was, I was afraid there would be *a donnybrook* if Daddy answered and had to come and pick me up. No way would he have let this joker off lightly for leaving his daughter alone for one second in isolated woods. Mr. Hot lips might have had some swell added to become Mr. Puffy Lips for a few days. I didn't want my father going to jail, so that option was out. And I didn't have cab money even if I could hike to the main road.

The only thing to do—start walking. The park was enormous, approximately 9,000 acres. Stranded in the middle of dead man's land, I realized I hadn't been paying attention to the back road turns. I normally had a good sense of direction but now disoriented, I felt fear settling into the marrow of my bones. I didn't really know John. I'd met him a few days before, and been assured by others who knew him he was a nice guy. Inside, my heart cried out, "Oh God, how could he? Is he ever coming back?"

With fear quickly subsiding, I thanked the Lord anger returned. My next thought: "If that joker comes back, I'm going to have some blood on *my* hands because I'm killing John myself. After I strangle him to make him suffer for a long slow while." That's when I heard the car engine rev. Two pranksters rolled up before me doubled over from laughter.

Hoping they choked, I was relieved John had returned, however, there was no relief that would cool my sizzling temper. Refraining from kicking his tires, I slid into the front seat red-hot mad. If I'd been wearing hot pants they would have burned a hole through the seat and melted clean through his chassis. The rest of that episode was shrouded in pure white vapor. I can only imagine John had to have plastic surgery on his right ear as I most likely chewed it raw by the time he dropped me off—for the last time. It's possible I could have said something along these lines: "Rip up the paper my phone number is on, eat the pieces, never call me again, and may you have heart burn the rest of your life. And if you park this car and leave it, you can count on me carving my name with a serrated grapefruit spoon in bold script on your leather seats."

Whatever I said, it worked. I never heard from "I'm-a-man-and-I-can't-help-but-love-you-so ever again." So much for love.

But oh, no. That didn't mean I was rid of The Joker. His family owned a business I drove past every day. And every day when I saw John's last name on the sign, I was reminded of a "last date." With The Joker. When John took over the family business and added his first name to the sign in big bold letters, I drove by thinking, "Well, well, the joker is now helping people instead of leaving them stranded. The wild child must have been tamed."

Which brings me back to Nashville many years later and my night on the internet watching a "coyote kill." The next day I let my daughter watch the video. Then I shared the story about my dates with hot lips John and how our budding friendship ended on a sour twang note.

Peyton laughed. "Mom, you've been holding a grudge against this guy for all of these years? That joke is as old as the hills! All young boys play that trick on girls."

Indignant, I tried to pretend I was cognizant of that "fact."

"Surely they don't play that trick on girls they *like*. Still, you don't leave a young girl alone in the woods. Even if it was broad daylight. Besides, in my heart, I forgave him a long time ago. I am *not* holding a grudge."

My daughter thought the story hilarious and wouldn't leave it alone. Still digging, she said, "Mom. He was a young boy. Come on! How long was John gone before he turned his car around to pick you up?"

I wanted to say 15 minutes but didn't want to double white lie so said, "Five." If I'm to be *totally* honest here, it was more like three. Long enough to go over the hill and turn around before driving back. But at the time, in the stone-cold stillness of those deep hooty-owl woods, three minutes seemed like dusk 'til dawn.

Still laughing, Peyton Googled John on Facebook. There was a family banner photo posted with the same young man who was the coyote hunter. "Look Mom, here's John. And Coyote Killer looks like maybe a grandson. And look at this other link. Here it says John has held a rodeo on his farm with all proceeds going to St. Jude Hospital for years. Sounds like a pretty good guy if you ask me."

Seriously? I preferred him a villain all these decades. Taking a closer look, I read where over one million dollars had been raised for the children of St. Jude over the last 16 years. I thought of my cousin's child who had been diagnosed at three years old with leukemia. St. Jude doctors had saved her life.

Had I ever been so hasty to misjudge John! He turned out to be a decent human being with some of the crazy wild ironed out. At the time of my perceived "abandonment," he was only a young boy full of fun and life playing practical jokes, never dreaming some girl he met at a party was going to get her britches bunched over a seemingly—to a teen boy—innocent prank. Fortunately or unfortunately, I'd never had a guy play that prank—most were trying to figure out how to finagle me *in* to their cars not in keeping me *out*. So, I'd had no clue what was happening. If I'd known about the joke, maybe I wouldn't have felt so helpless and frightened—knowing his intent all along was to quickly return.

And in the heat of the moment, when John saw how upset I was, surely he apologized. Why couldn't I remember? Even if he *had* apologized, I hadn't yet developed the skills needed to talk things through to move past our first fracas and onto true friendship. I simply wanted *away* from what I perceived as treachery. All my young mind could process was, "If he left me stranded, how else will he betray me?" Like Dorothy in the Wizard of Oz, I only wanted to go home. But I wasn't as strong as Dorothy or as bold and adventurous on *my* yellow brick road.

Besides, Dorothy's adventure was no more than a dream. My adventure was for scary real. I was actually in the woods alone facing lions, tigers, and bears—oh, no! Okay, I'm overreaching a bit here. And maybe I had overreacted years ago.

Alright, I had.

After my daughter-mother lecture I drove back to Chattanooga and there was John's name in my face again. Once more I head-heard, "John left me stranded on a national battlefield. Epic." Perhaps Peyton was right and I had been holding onto a grudge. But how could I change this instant replay script?

More bad memories flooded in. This time, of Peyton totaling her SUV at this same spot on I-24 while in a drizzling rain on the way to school. Her caved-in vehicle had traffic backed up to Cleveland, Tennessee until the wreckage could be removed. The policeman at the hospital told me he'd never seen anyone survive a crash so horrendous.

Informed the SUV had been towed by a wrecker and towing service and could be found on their lot, the officer added, "Don't go. It's really bad. One of the worst I've ever seen." Of course, I had to go to see what my child had been pulled out of.

But there lay the rub. I might be forced to face John. All of my adult life I'd avoided this man. Then, he'd unknowingly performed a favor for me.

I learned even more eerie details. After Peyton's car passed over the ridge crest on I-24, the front tire had been caught by the lane divider. The vehicle flipped into a long slide down the interstate—tennis rackets, backpacks, books, and broken glass trailing behind. It finally stopped almost in front of and parallel to John's business.

I processed this scenario and glanced at the name on the wreckers in the parking lot, thinking, "I'm constantly bombarded with the ghost of this guy wherever I go. Can I *never, ever* get this guy out of my life?" I snapped a few quick photos of the wreck and thought about going inside to speak with John, but chickened out because for the life of me, I could not remember how that last date ended. How I'd gotten home. For the most part, I had blanked out the parting conversation or lack thereof. Most likely I'd ridden in doorknob dead silence refusing to give him another exhaled breath. Just how coyote ugly had I been?

The humorous part in all this angst was, since my name wasn't painted in large letters on a major building and I kept myself out of the newspapers, John had probably forgotten I existed. Only a twinkle in his vast universe, I doubted he recalled my name, the smokin' hot kiss, or the joke that went awry.

Decades later, the joke was probably still on me while John joyously ambled through life most likely unscathed from our childhood encounters.

Fast forward again as I now drove past John's business, I couldn't help but think of John 7:24: *Do not judge by appearances, but judge with right judgment.*

But here's the verse that popped into my head that slayed me. *When ye stand praying, forgive, if ye have ought against any: that your Father also which is in heaven may forgive you your trespasses.* Mark 11:25

Was my daughter right? Did I have "ought" against John and was I still holding a grudge against the boy of yesteryear while white lying about it—even to myself?

I knew that as a Christian I was to *be kind to one another, tenderhearted, forgiving one another, as God in Christ forgave you.* Ephesians 4:32

For after all, hadn't *I* been seen to be the worthy one—the chosen one—to repeat the lines of Mary and swaddle Jesus in the church play? Hadn't *I* been steeped in the Word of God since a child? Of all people, *I* knew better than to judge.

I could say my defining moment of the day was driving by John's place of business for the umpteenth time and experiencing God's truth again colliding with my thoughts: *The word of God* is *quick, and powerful, and sharper than any twoedged sword, piercing even to the dividing asunder of soul and spirit, and of the joints and marrow, and* is *a discerner of the thoughts and intents of the heart.* Hebrews 4:12

Acquainted with God's way of making it hard on a recalcitrant child, I said, "Okay God. I get it. I give. I'll try to lay the aggravating memories to rest and try to create good memories. I'll contact John, apologize to him for misjudging him all these years, thank him for supporting St. Jude Hospital which helped save my family member, and thank him for hauling Peyton's scrap metal off the streets. Let's just hope you prepare his heart in case he does remember the last date in detail and it was coyote ugly, he's in a good frame of mind, and doesn't get coyote ugly in return by coming to call with a grapefruit spoon.

The rest of the story...

I dragged my feet about contacting John and dreaded the conversation, certain he wouldn't remember me. But after so many coincidences, for instance: Genealogy work—the book I needed was written by a man with John's last name. I needed to find a humane way to kill coyotes... A week later at a Precept Ministries Bible study—a preacher's wife I'd never before met from Ringgold, Georgia sat down. The odds of that happening? Slim to none. My face almost fell in my chicken salad. So rattled was I over that incident I later went to the theatre to see a WWII movie—*Fury*—starring Brad Pitt. One of the main characters was from North Georgia. Two coincidences in one day? I choked on my popcorn when I heard the character say, "*North Georgia.*" I felt I was in a barrage of John's machine gun fire. Would I next be swallowed by a big fish if I didn't make the phone call? *Lord, can you at least tell me what this is all about before I make a fool of myself?*

I finally contacted John to apologize for any emotional pain I might have inflicted and to offer an olive branch. And as I had surmised, he didn't remember me or recall pranking me on the battlefield. In fact he said, "Are you sure it wasn't one of my brothers?" Really *mwah-hah-ha* epic!

After a moment of laughter and relief on my part that I hadn't scarred *him* for life, John gave me a re-boot on his latest escapades.

He married, had three children, lost a son in a car accident, and later adopted another child. The August rodeo on his farm to benefit St. Jude Hospital emerged from his love of horses and equine sports. Not only does he hold an annual rodeo, he schedules barrel racing and other events throughout the year in his covered arena and also competes, with the proceeds from the rodeo going to St. Jude. "I'll do anything to help these kids," he told me.

Now *that* is true love.

At last I had a new head tape to play every time I passed by John's business. And I was convinced that John could honestly sing the song about love for which I'd long ago associated him with: "I'm a Man."

No doubt, that benevolent and can't-help-but-love-you-so man is still a "little joker." Some things never change.

❧ 35 ❧
Never Judge an Orange by the Fuzz

Why would I dream about a man with greyhounds? Wracking my brain, I finally remembered.

I'd visited Rugby, Tennessee to experience what Christmas would have been like in a "utopian" village built for younger sons of Englishmen who didn't stand a chance of inheriting their father's wealth. The primogeniture laws were clear: To keep lands and estates intact, the bulk of the inheritance was handed down to the eldest son. Therefore, in 1880 British author Thomas Hughes had purchased land in the mountains of Tennessee and founded Rugby colony—an experimental utopian colony—so these younger sons would at last have an occupation. A cannery was built to can tomatoes the sons would grow. The experiment was destined to fail for the most part. The young Englishmen had lived lives of leisure. The hard work of growing, gathering, and canning tomatoes held no interest for them. The gallants enjoyed horse games, leisurely picnics with friends, and fishing mountain streams.

In the 1960s, a small community still lingered and friends, residents, and descendants of Rugby began restoring the original design and layout of the colony. When I heard about Rugby, I was intrigued and had to go experience the community for myself. I was all in for "stepping back in time."

While at Rugby during a Christmas tour I had snapped a photo of a bearded Father Christmas wearing a blue velvet robe trimmed in white, escorted by two adoring greyhounds. We never spoke. Father Christmas was acting out his part for the event and I was headed for the next home tour to see how people lived in the late 1800s. After my tour, I headed for the community center and a cup of hot cider wassail to warm up, never dreaming this frigid night would trigger a dream months later.—A dream of a stranger wearing nondescript clothes surrounded by greyhounds. Or was the dream triggered by something else? Was there a bigger picture?

A couple of verses in the Bible have always intrigued me. Joel 2:28-29: *It shall come to pass afterward, that I will pour out My Spirit upon all flesh; and your sons and your daughters shall prophesy, your old men shall dream dreams, your young men shall see visions. And also upon the servants and upon the handmaids in those days will I pour out My Spirit.*

Three days after my odd dream of the man with the greyhounds, I attended a writing conference in Tennessee. This conference had been on my calendar for months. During the "meet and greet" cocktail party, I noticed a man, wearing overalls and sporting a full beard, ease through the door. This was either his first time to a writing conference and he didn't know that writers usually gussied up for the "meet and greet," or he was simply an honest, hard working man and a pair of overalls was what he felt most comfortable wearing. Perhaps this pair of overalls was all he owned.

The would-be writer stood by himself, totally ignored, with me wondering why some of the men didn't welcome him to the party and conference. What to do? I was hesitant about approaching men I didn't know without first being introduced. Yet, I couldn't let him stand there by himself, all forlorn looking and seemingly out of place.

I'd been reared in the city during the week, however, I'd spent summers and weekends on my family's farms where I was "raised." Plus, I now lived on 45 acres and had a hunter jumper riding school. If I had a need to, I could carry on a conversation about horses and livestock. I could even tell a few yarns about soybeans, corn, and other crops along with how incredible burgers were at an Alabama stockyard sale for cattle, horses, and mules. But first, I had to get over my hesitancy of meeting a gentleman without first being introduced. *You can do this.* Okay God. Help me walk on over there.

"Hi. I'm Vicki. Is this your first time to attend this conference?"

"It is—I'm Fuzzy Orange."

I couldn't help but laugh which is what he was, no doubt, expecting.

"Come on, your parents named you Fuzzy Orange?" Thinking back on that eventful meeting, Fuzzy probably thought I was extremely rude. But I was thinking, *Now, here, is a man with stories.*

"It's on my driver's license. I once had a cop pull me over. He took one look at my name and shook his head. 'No way your name is Fuzzy Orange.'" Fuzzy had taken my teasing in good stride.

"Well, Fuzzy Orange, what brings you here? Tell me a little about yourself. What do you write?" My interest was definitely piqued and Fuzzy seemed like an old soul who'd never met a stranger. If only the others keeping their distance would look beyond the overalls and rambling fuzzy beard to have a chat with him.

Fuzzy continued, "I have a lot of stories I'd like to write down. I also rescue greyhounds off the race track."

"You've come to the right place...Wait a minute—you say you rescue greyhounds?" I tried not to choke on my cracker and cheddar. "No way! I *dreamed* about you *three nights ago*!" I slammed down a sip of water so I wouldn't blow cracker dust all over Mr. Fuzzy's wild and wooly beard. "Wait another second—were you ever at Rugby, Tennessee dressed up like Father Christmas with your greyhounds?"

Fuzzy grinned, his eyes twinkling. He stuck both hands inside his overall bib. Rocked back on his heels and then back again before saying, "That would be me."

My exuberant outburst gained the entire room's attention. Those who'd paid Fuzzy no mind until then, gathered around this gentle man and listened in on our conversation.

"I can hardly believe this," I said. "I have a photo of you in your long blue-hooded robe with your greyhounds. I found it after my dream about you, though I didn't know it was you. I've been staring at that photo for three days thinking, *What's up with my being mesmerized by this photo?* We definitely were meant to meet. Now we must find out why. I'll help you figure out the conference workshops if you need help, Fuzzy. I'm so glad you came."

Once Fuzzy had everyone's attention and a small crowd surrounded us, someone nearby told me, "Don't worry about Fuzzy, Vicki, I'll take good care of him from here on out." I couldn't help but wonder, *Where were you when Fuzzy needed someone to talk to before now? You left him standing all by himself, ignored, when it was obvious he should have been warmly welcomed and made to feel at home. And now you want to be Fuzzy's best friend because suddenly he sounds extremely interesting?*

Maybe I was making too much out of it. Not wanting to make waves, I placed Fuzzy into someone else's care with reluctance. And I wondered about my dream about him. Surely my dream and randomly coming across the photo I'd taken of him, along with his attending the same writers conference—were not coincidences. Had God intentionally given me the dream to help pave the way for Fuzzy to feel at home at the conference? The Lord was up to something if only I could figure out what that something was.

The next day, I couldn't help but wonder how Fuzzy was getting along. I hoped people were treating him well. He wasn't in any of the workshops I attended and I had no way of knowing how he'd fared.

After a couple of days zoomed by I—along with others—was looking forward to the awards banquet dinner. Arriving in the banquet room a tad early to save a table for a few friends running fashionably late, I chose my seat. I noticed one of the tables near the speaker's podium was already taken by the person who had placed Fuzzy "under his wing." Yet, he'd saved no extra dinner seat for Fuzzy. Then I heard the gentle man's voice behind me, "Vicki, mind if I sit at your table?"

Fuzzy still wore the same pair of overalls he'd arrived in while the other men wore suits and ties. "Sure, Fuzzy. That seat right there has your name on it." After we all finished off our strawberry cheesecake, Fuzzy said, "Vicki, if you'll come out to my car, I have something I'd like to give you."

Hmmmm. What to do? I wasn't sure about the invitation or the surprise gift but said, "Okay" because I didn't want to offend Fuzzy.

In the dimly lit parking lot, Fuzzy opened his car trunk. *Oh no. I don't really know this guy. Is that a gleam I see in his eye? What if he's a serial killer beneath his Father Christmas shtick and throws me in his trunk and screeches off?* Then I saw it. Fuzzy pulled a long stick from his trunk.

Oh Lord! Is Fuzzy going to beat me with a stick? To later cut me up into little pieces for greyhound dog food? News headlines flashed through my mind: "Tennessee Writer's Body Found—well, all but the flesh. Nothing left but a bag of bones and a skull with missing teeth. She was kidnapped after being beaten senseless, thrown into the trunk of Fuzzy Orange's vehicle, and later succumbed to a wood chipper to become ground dog food for Father Christmas's rescued greyhounds."

I know. Funny what I thought about before my probable death. Writers—at least this one—tend to be drama queens and melodramatic. But there was that time I was stalked at the mall, and the other time when….

Right when I thought the worst was going to happen and I might have to actually use a Karate move I'd learned in college, Fuzzy grinned and said, "This here, is a 'Fuzzy Stick.'"

A nervous hiccup slipped out before I could ask, "What do you do with a Fuzzy stick?"

"When I clear the fence rows of young saplings at home, I make these walking sticks. I'd like to give you one for being so nice and helping me at this conference." On the shellacked stick was burned: "Fuzzy Stick—Fence Row 2008." I was never so honored, humbled, and ashamed for previously thinking the worst about Fuzzy's trunk and intentions. And relieved I wasn't going to be the next meal for Fuzzy's beloved greyhounds. The mind can race from zero to crazy in a heartbeat. But now, I couldn't thank this kind and generous man enough.

Years later, Fuzzy once again popped into my mind. I attempted to locate him anew to determine if he'd published his stories but couldn't find him on Facebook, nor could I find a Fuzzy Orange anywhere on the internet.

After a major move I ran across his photo again—all dressed up as Father Christmas—and propped it up on my desk, still wondering about Fuzzy's whereabouts. But why? Why was I thinking about Fuzzy Orange? The dream. Three nights before the writing conference. There was the number three again. The number three frequently pops up in the Bible. The Trinity—God, Jesus, and the Holy Spirit. Three wise men bringing three gifts for the baby Jesus. Why not a baker's dozen of wise men? Jonah was in the belly of the big fish three days. The list goes on and on.

While I was pondering all of this, I read an article by an anonymous writer. She'd written about hotdogs and jotted down a few of her words on paper: "Does today's hotdog coincidence/ twilight zone event mean someone is going to give me a hotdog related gift soon? Maybe a year's supply of chili or perhaps free stents due to high cholesterol?" My mind drifted. "Fuzzy, if you're out there, I'm really enjoying my walking stick! FUZZY—are you out there? There is now a band named Fuzzy Orange—I wonder if they met the real Fuzzy? *Or is that Fuzzy's band?* FUZZEEE! Where are you?" *Why did my mind just zip on over to Fuzzy Orange from hotdogs?*

I told my grandchildren about this humble man named Fuzzy Orange and showed them my "Fuzzy Stick." Tickled, they, too, giggled about Fuzzy's name and wondered who would name a baby, Fuzzy Orange?

Finally, one day I heard in my spirit, *check out the obits for Fuzzy*. Why hadn't I thought of that before? I finally found my long lost friend in the 2019 online obits. "Harley Clay 'Fuzzy' Orange." Fuzzy was a nickname. I deduced from my high school French that Fuzzy was probably of French descent and his ancestors were more than likely of the de Orange family and one of the followers of William, Duke of Normandy or possibly he was distantly related to William of Orange, king of England from 1688 to 1702. The name "Orange" was also found in England as a surname of Huguenot origin.

From working on genealogy, I knew that some Huguenots left Europe for America and settled in ten of the colonies but especially in a North Carolina community before some, more than likely, made their way into Tennessee via Revolutionary War land grants. At least Fuzzy Orange's last name now made more sense. I continued reading the obituary:

"A Navy veteran, Fuzzy started college at 65 years old and traveled the world building homes with Habitat for Humanity.

He shook hands with several presidents."

I located the preacher who'd officiated at Fuzzy's funeral. Perhaps he knew if Fuzzy had successfully written his stories. If so, I'd purchase his book. I was in luck when the preacher answered his phone. After I explained my mission, he said, "Fuzzy was quite the character and he and his wife—she'd passed before him—were members of the church where I preached before retiring. He never published his stories. He'd asked me to read a couple of them but they still needed work.

"Fuzzy, however, once told me a tale about building homes for the poor in South Africa. He felt a tap on his shoulder and when he turned around, Nelson Mandela was standing there saying, 'Thank you.' He then shook Fuzzy's hand. Now, when I tell people about Fuzzy, I say, 'I shook the hand of the man who shook the hand of Nelson Mandela.'"

Now, I can say that too.

RIP Fuzzy. You still hold a warm place in my heart, a heart that was—unbeknownst to you—greatly touched by your sweet soul. There was so much more to you than what most gathered upon first glance. You were loved. And I'm so glad God prepared my heart to meet you at the conference and help pave the way for you to be accepted. See you again real soon. And hey, save me a place in your storytelling corner of heaven. Meet you on the giggle cloud.

Funny, as I finish typing the last sentence of this story, I'm smelling the scent of—oranges.

Fuzzy, is that you?

～ 36 ～
Paying Peonies Forward

Sometimes I wonder if God gets tired of my complaining. And the song comes to mind, "Why Me Lord? What have I ever done...."

Of course, I know what I've done. The Holy Spirit is quick to remind me of everything I've ever done including stealing a piece of Double Bubble gum from the grocery store when I was four years old while Mother was in the checkout line paying for a buggy load of groceries.

Another time I was ashamed of myself was when Mother asked me to drive to her home and dig up all of her peonies and divide them. I thought, *Oh, nice! It's been longer than three years since she planted them and it's time they were divided and I'll get some of her peonies to plant in my garden.*

But the excitement waned when Mother added, "I want to give the divided peony tubers to friends."

"What?! You want me to do the hard labor of digging up those big bushy plants that by now have spread out roots all the way to the next county, divide them, for you to give to your friends and other family members—like the 'friend' who you allowed to take a shovel to your well established hosta?

The same 'friend,' who instead of digging up the entire plants, sliced through the hosta midway with a rounded shovel making your plants look like half-moon-pies—ruining the look of your landscaping?"

I was on a roll and couldn't cease and desist. "Your hosta plants look hideous out there. I can't believe you didn't tell her to dig up the entire hosta plants, divide, and replant! The same 'friend' who pulls her feet up to your dinner table for a good meal on a regular basis but rarely cooks for you or invites you and Daddy to her and her husband's house?" I sucked in a deep breath to better chide.

"You're always doing for everybody else, Mother. You need to stop letting other people take advantage of you." I was on a righteous rolling rant.

Mother stayed silent. I knew she wasn't able to dig up the peonies or she would have done it herself. She'd rather do a job herself than ask for help. And I knew that there were some friends and family who were "more needy" than others—which translates to "lazy and cheap"—and you simply helped them anyway because some of them were just plain selfish but you loved them just the same. That's life 101. And part of being a Christ follower is to be a cheerful giver. Give and you shall receive—I'd heard that a thousand times. However, Mother was rarely on the receiving end. She was a do-gooder, as Daddy called her. And he was quick to remind her of the time she took a cake to a sick neighbor's house and the woman's German Shepherd waited until Mother got upon the porch and bit her smack dab on the derriere. "Her bottom looked like chewed hamburger for weeks!" Daddy said, chuckling. "All because she's a do-gooder."

I sighed. I'd given more than a piece of my mind, I'd given a pie-shaped wedge. Rant over.

"Okay, Mother. Next time I'm down, I'll dig up peonies and get the job done for you."

Why couldn't I have said that in the first place rather than vent about selfish people who used her?

Now, I had a big job before me. Not only would I have to dig up the peonies and divide them, I'd have to label the peonies so the colors wouldn't get mixed up because I was sure someone ungratefully receiving a free peony tuber would say, "I don't like pink peonies, I only like the white ones. Why didn't you give me the white ones? That bush bloomed out pink blooms! Pink doesn't go with my garden color scheme. I wanted the Festiva Maxima tubers—the one that has that red drizzled through the center of the bloom!"

Heaven forbid a friend taking home a free peony tuber and a year later discovering the blooming peony flower turned out to be pink. *Pink! Can you imagine, pink! She knows I'm a red kinda girl.*

After I hung up the phone, I continued playing the silent rant in my head. I would be doing all of the digging, dividing, and labeling, I would then have to prepare the ground to replant Mother's portion of the divided peonies. Such a huge job when I had plenty of gardening work to do in my own garden. I'd been fighting a Japanese beetle infestation and spraying frequently and I was afraid I was going to lose my ornamental trees. Now, another chore added to my ever-growing list. And furthermore, the horse stalls needed cleaning out. The dogs had ear mites. Blah. Blah. Blah.

Then the guilt hit.

Again, I knew Mother wouldn't have asked me to do all of this digging if she could pick up a shovel and hop to it. Daddy had his hands full taking care of his cattle and the rest of the farm. Plus, Daddy didn't know a peony tuber eye from a purple yam eye because he'd never grown either one. He knew absolutely nothing about dividing peonies. Why couldn't I do this one job without all of the whining and maundering? Mother didn't ask for much and she'd helped me often when I needed a babysitter and help with one big move.

There were times in the fall when the mountains caught on fire and threatened to destroy every home and barn around and when I got the phone call from Mother and Daddy to come help, I didn't mind driving to my parents' farm to fight fires to keep their property from devastation and everything they owned from being destroyed. I dropped all I was doing. If I had horses in the ring, I yanked saddles off and turned the horses out to pasture, hopped in the car, and raced to their home.

Once there, I was ready to help rake away leaves near the fence lines that needed to be cleared so flames couldn't jump over into the pasture from the woods to then burn down outbuildings. And more. We'd always helped one another.

And I really appreciated the canned green beans, tomatoes, and soup stock Mother sent home with me. My parents were loving and incredible parents and grandparents, so why was I all bent out of shape over dividing peony bulbs? Was it because of the weeds that had crowded up close to the plants to make the job more difficult? Or, was it because I wasn't getting my fair share of the tubers after doing all of the heavy lifting and back-breaking work?

That was definitely part of it. Peonies were my favorites. I thought surely Mother would give me a few. But the other part was definitely because Mother allowed herself to be taken advantage of by a couple of relatives and friends who asked for what seemed like—everything.

After I finished the peony job, I never asked Mother where the peony tubers ended up. I decided giving those peony tubers away was something she enjoyed immensely. She simply enjoyed giving gifts. And she never waited for someone to do something for her, she was always the first to give and share what she had. That's why she was so loved and why later, 300 people showed up at the funeral home to stand in a toad-strangler-rain until they could get inside to pay their respect.

So, I let that peony-dividing resentment go. Families and friends had enough issues to be divided over and I decided a bloomin' peony wasn't going to be a dividing issue.

After Mother had a heart attack and later broke her leg and couldn't tend to her plants like she'd always done when she was younger, I became head gardener—the only gardener—of not only my property but my parents' property as well.

Did I have to give up other interests of my own to help take care of two farms instead of one? Absolutely. But did I mind giving up those things? Absolutely not. I was saddened to give up my horses but I'd rather enjoy my parents for as long as I could and help make them happy because I knew they wouldn't always be around to visit with and I cherished our fireside chats. I loved to sit in an ancestor's rocking chair in front of my parents' floor to ceiling fireplace while reading newspaper articles—one that made me laugh so hard one time, I slid out of the rocking chair onto the carpet in a puddle of my own making while catching Mother's comment, "Vicki, you make me want to live." I wanted my parents to live forever. I dreaded the day it would be time for them to go to their heavenly home.

So, I joyfully replanted tulip bulbs in one of Mother's large planters. Around the birdbath in the backyard, I planted pansies every year in the fall, and in the spring, I planted annuals. I mowed the extensive lawn. I helped by trimming shrubs. I washed the car and took it for new tires when needed.

When a winter's freeze killed all of Mother's azaleas, I bought a truck load of azalea bushes and delivered them for a workday gathering beneath the pines in the side yard close to the mountain bluff.

One day, after I'd tirelessly worked at planting the flowers I'd bought to spruce up the flower bed around Mother's birdbath Daddy said, "Why do you go to the trouble to plant flowers here every year?" I replied, "Because Mother enjoys them and perhaps it will help perk her up since she can no longer lift and dig to keep her flower beds tidy. It has to be more pleasing to walk by the great room window and look out on colorful flowers than to look out on ugly weeds, don't you agree Daddy?"

"I guess. You just work so hard planting everything."

Soon afterwards, Daddy approved climbing roses to be planted—something I'd mentioned several years earlier. I've written before about driving to the Rose Emporium in Georgia north of Atlanta to buy climbing roses that Mother would see when she passed in front of the floor-to-ceiling window in the great room—and how that road trip almost cost me my life.

However, that trip was worth the scare. All turned out well. And I'm forever reminded of the words of the Apostle Paul: *Let us not be weary in well doing: for in due season we shall reap, if we faint not.* Galatians 6:9

That's the key. Not fainting. Staying strong for as long as possible to be available to share and do for others. Not only sharing material things, but the love of Christ and the Good News that there's salvation and eternal life through Him.

Who knows? Perhaps the recipients of the peony tubers have now divided their peonies and passed the love forward. For "paying it forward" is always the best way. Sharing is caring and keeps the heart healthy in more ways than one.

One thing for sure, when I get to heaven and I'm possibly asked, "What have you ever done...?" I can say, "I divided peony tubers once even though I didn't plan on getting my fair share." And if asked, "But did you dig and divide those peony tubers with a happy and joyful heart or were you grumpy and resentful which might just cancel out your good deed?" I will reply, "Oh, dear St. Peter, at first, I was definitely grumpy and resentful—you're sometimes that way with the ones you love the most, don't you remember when you were down on Earth—but I finally got to the point where I tried harder every day to be joyful and cheerful no matter what I was asked to do. Does trying count?"

I imagine I hear Jesus who is full of grace say, "You have fought the good fight and finished the race all the while keeping your faith—I think I can forgive your fuss and bother over digging up a few peony tubers without a cut. Let her in St. Peter. And welcome to heaven my child."

I can't wait until I meet Jesus face to face so I can tell Him, "Thank you Lord, lover of my soul, for mercy and your invaluable gift—grace."

...being justified freely by His grace through the redemption that is in Christ Jesus. Romans 3:24

As many as walk according to this rule, peace be on them, and mercy, and upon the Israel of God. Galatians 6:16

About The Author

VICKI H. Moss is former Editor-at-Large and Contributing Editor for *Southern Writers Magazine* where she interviewed authors and contributed articles on writing in addition to blogging for the magazine's Suite T blog. She also wrote a weekly column as a pundit for the *American Daily Herald*. As a workshop instructor for writing conferences, Vicki teaches from her books *How to Write for Kids' Magazines* and *Writing with Voice*.

With over 800 published articles, she co-authored the book *nailed It!* and contributed to Cecil Murphey's book, *I Believe in Heaven*. A poet, blogger, speaker, free-lance editor, and ghostwriter, Vicki is frequently on faculty as a workshop instructor along with school author visits. She's also author of *Adrift, Smelling Stinkweed, Rogue Hearts,* and two poetry books *Roisin Dubh* and *Porch Pickin' People*— and always has a work in progress. Writing for many venues, she's published articles and poems in Scotland's *Thistle Blower, Country Woman, Christian Devotions, In the City, Hopscotch, Fun for Kidz, Boys' Quest,* and has written over 40 stories for the Moments series published by Grace Publishing.

Find Vicki at the following:
www.livingwaterfiction.com
Instagram @vickihmoss
X @VickiMoss

Enjoy!

www.ingramcontent.com/pod-product-compliance
Lightning Source LLC
Chambersburg PA
CBHW062203080426
42734CB00010B/1772